Praise for *Scary Good*

Part memoir, part master class, *Scary Good* is written with refreshing, laugh-out-loud honesty. Angie Callen shares her personal and professional challenges — and the solutions she discovered along the way — to inspire us to live our values and our purpose. Readers will see themselves in every chapter.

Carol Lin, Emmy Award–Winning Journalist and Author of *When News Breaks: A Memoir of Love and War*

Angie Callen writes like she coaches — no BS, all heart, and with the kind of wisdom that only comes from actually living it. *Scary Good* is a field guide for anyone who's ever felt the gap between who they are and what they do for a living, written by someone who's navigated real-life detours and come out the other side more aligned — and funnier — than ever. If you've ever felt like you're succeeding on paper but suffocating in practice, Angie's story will make you laugh, her frameworks will make you think, and her message will make you brave enough to build the life you actually want.

Mike Kim, *Wall Street Journal* Best-Selling Author of *You Are the Brand*

Angie Callen blends practical wisdom, wit, charm, and grit in an engaging adventure. I loved how she made me feel like I was evolving along with her on the sometimes bumpy but always educational road of life, celebrating its most unlikely gifts.

Diane M. Simard, Life Commentator and Author of *Unlikely Gifts Unwrapped*

As a leadership coach and self-care advocate, I found *Scary Good* to be a breath of fresh air for anyone who's ever let "Monday ruin their Sunday." Angie Callen blends honesty, humor, and hard-won wisdom to remind us that alignment — not hustle — is the antidote to burnout. This isn't another productivity pep talk; it's a compassionate call to be human again.

Joyel Crawford, Award-Winning Executive Coach, Speaker, and Author of *Show Your Ass*

Scary Good is a brave, unputdownable reminder that we're never stuck — we're becoming. Angie Callen shows us how to find hope, meaning, and reinvention in the messy middle of life.

Gina Riley, Author of *Qualified Isn't Enough* and Creator of Career Velocity™

If you've ever felt your Sundays fill with dread because of the upcoming workweek (and who hasn't?), then *Scary Good* is an absolute must-read. Angie Callen describes her professional and personal journey in a way that feels authentic, vulnerable, and deeply relatable — and it's bursting with personality and charm. But let me be clear: this book isn't just a memoir. It's as outward-facing as it is inward-facing, offering brilliant insights, rich reflection exercises, and practical resources for readers who want real change. *Scary Good* is inspiring and transformative.

Greg Chasson, Psychologist, Professor at the University of Chicago, and Author of *Flawed: Why Perfectionism Is a Challenge for Management*

As someone who built a business after 40, I know firsthand that the path to success isn't always linear — and it shouldn't cost you your peace. Angie's *Scary Good* isn't just another career book; it's a permission slip to design your life with intention instead of letting Sunday anxiety dictate your worth. What resonates most is her message that our work should align with our values, not suffocate them. You don't have to choose between success and fulfillment — you can have both when you're brave enough to trust your intuition and build something authentic. This book is for anyone who's ever felt trapped by what they "should" be doing instead of what they're called to do.

Keenya Kelly, Visibility Coach and Author of *Before You Quit Your Job*

Holy smokes! This book is so relatable yet so eye-opening. Angie is the new Stephanie Plum of self-help. I'll definitely put this book to good use, breaking out of my own Type A-perfectionism box.

Christine James, DO, Physician and Associate Professor

Scary Good does not try to fix you. It tells the truth about what happens when your life looks right on paper but feels wrong in your body. Angie captures the tension between success and fulfillment in a way that is rare and refreshing. She has a gift for saying the things people feel but rarely say out loud. If you've ever felt the weight of Sundays without knowing why, this book will help you understand what your discomfort is pointing toward. Having spent decades measuring my worth by titles and outcomes, then stepping into self-employment, this book hit home in a deeper way than I expected. In an AI-driven world, that shift is not optional — it is our moat.

Liam Darmody, Brand Strategist and Business Innovation Coach

Angie's advice on how to build alignment with your own personal version of success is simple and relatable. As somebody who also spent years climbing the professional ladder only to realize it didn't lead to a meaningful or satisfying life, I appreciate her wise and practical tips on how to skip those years of stress and heartbreak.

Eric Nehrlich, Executive Coach and Author of *You Have a Choice*

Scary Good feels like sitting with a wise older friend who isn't afraid to tell the truth about how scary, how hard, how messy, and how beautiful growth can be. Angie's story echoes so many of my own twists and turns, and in reading her reflections, I found myself rewriting my own narratives through her fresh lenses of leadership and authenticity. If you're wondering what's possible outside the 9–5, this book is an invitation to self-trust and to believe in the bigger life that's calling to you.

Amber Jackson, Executive Coach and CEO

Leaders often fear that one failure will define them forever, but Angie Callen proves that resilience isn't about bouncing back to what was — it's about building something new. Through honest storytelling and hard-earned clarity, she shows what it means to move from living by default to living by design. *Scary Good* is a field guide drawn from personal fire and from coaching thousands of professionals and entrepreneurs through their own pivots. It offers a clear roadmap for anyone staring down the Sunday Scaries and navigating a transition phase. An inspirational read for "the burnt out, the brave, and everyone in between."

Christoff Poppe, CEO Coach and Vistage Chair

Scary Good is the kind of book that makes you exhale and say, *finally someone is telling the truth* about how hard it is to build a life that actually feels like yours. Angie writes with the kind of honesty and insight that cuts through the noise and helps you see yourself more clearly. As someone who has spent years teaching people how to trust themselves at work, I found this book to be a refreshing reminder that the voice we most often ignore is our own. *Scary Good* isn't just a read, it's a reset.

Neelu Kaur, Speaker, Organizational Psychologist, and Author of *Be Your Own Cheerleader*

This book is perfect for anyone who feels the ache of wanting more meaning, purpose, and success. It's filled with powerful insights and tools to help you step into the driver's seat of your life to get those things. With a balance of wisdom and humor, Angie takes readers on an exploration of what truly matters. Her candid approach speaks directly to the things that hold us back, and she shows us how to reframe the stories that keep us stuck.

Terri Maxwell, Investor, Business Growth Expert, and Founder of Share On Purpose, Inc.

I'm more of a Mon-Yay type of girl, but Angie's book applies to all of us who find ourselves stuck clinging to the safe places — where every dream remains just a silly dream. If you've been taking your F.I.N.E., fine meds, you might want to start detoxing with each chapter of *Scary Good*.

Stef Layton, RYT-500 (Registered Yoga Teacher)

Scary Good is a refreshing blend of memoir and motivation that invites you to rethink how you show up in life and work. Angie's story of resilience and living life on her own terms resonated deeply and prompted reflection on my own journey. Her humor, honesty, and soul-shifting insights — especially in Chapter 11 — made me feel seen and encouraged. This book is perfect for anyone navigating burnout, questioning their path, or needing permission to simply be themselves.

Dustin Beasley, Career Coach and Founder of Career Renovators

Angie's debut is a refreshingly honest reminder that our paths are never set in stone, and that the courage to take a switchback can lead us exactly where we need to be. With vulnerability, humor, and lived wisdom, she shows us that failure is really opportunity in disguise. Anyone looking to design their life with intention — not just work a job — needs this honest, human, and deeply relatable book.

Lindsay Harle-Kadatz Speaker, Coach, and Quirky Human

Scary Good is honest, funny, and full of moments that make you rethink the stories you tell yourself. I loved Angie's reminder that identity is so much more than the labels we pick up along the way, and that the people (and pets!) who walk with us, whether for a season or a lifetime, shape us in powerful ways. Her story made me reflect on my own, especially as a forty-something woman redefining what I want next. It's warm, real, and laugh-out-loud funny — perfect for anyone who wants a little joy with their existential reckoning.

Lindi Bolinger, Travel Coach and Founder of Wander•On Journeys

In *Scary Good: Discovering Life Beyond the Sunday Scaries*, Angie Callen leads us on an adventure to a more aligned self, one where we're no longer dreading Sunday evenings and the coming work week, but excited to see what opportunities await us.

With humor and vulnerability, Angie paves the way for us to take a hard, honest look at our lives, determine what's working and what isn't — just as she has. Then she invites us to discover a new way of being — aligned, authentic, and true to the very core of who we are.

Whether you are employed or forging into the world as an entrepreneur, *Scary Good* is for you. Angie's life story serves as a reminder that you are worth every ounce of happiness, success, and fulfillment that you desire.

Kathy Sparrow, The Literary Midwife, and author of *The Whispered Teachings of Grandmother Trout*

This book moved me in ways I didn't expect. It brought tears to my eyes and made me laugh out loud, but most importantly, I felt a deep connection as I followed Angie's journey. So many moments mirrored my own growth, especially in building confidence and trusting myself as I continue to learn and evolve. Angie's story inspired me to keep moving forward with courage, both personally and professionally. As a coach and a leader, I walked away feeling more grounded, more hopeful, and more confident in who I am becoming. A powerful, heartfelt read that stays with you long after you close the last page.

Stephanie Renk, Master Job Search Coach and Founder of Next Step Career Services

As someone whose career has also taken unexpected — and far more fulfilling — turns, I loved every word of *Scary Good: Discovering Life Beyond the Sunday Scaries*. Many of us know the feeling of dreading the workweek, but not everyone takes action to change it. If you feel life and career are happening to you instead of something you make happen, Angie Callen's memoir is for you. With warmth, humor, and humility, she shares her journey from corporate burnout to meaningful work, practical strategies for trusting your instincts, and stories of reinvention that feel both inspiring and achievable. It's wisdom every working human needs to hear.

Anna Schardt Baker, Founder and President of Three Story Strategies, LLC

You will laugh. You will cry. You will learn a bit about Angie and even more about yourself with every turn of the page. Angie reminds us that equilibrium, contentment, and peace — the welcome byproducts of our roller coaster lives — are what living a *Scary Good* life is truly about, and that they are not as elusive as we might think.

Ben Wiant, Outdoor Adventurer, Husband, and Career Consultant

If you've stalled out in your career and feel like there's something more for you in life, then you're right. *Scary Good* is Angie Callen's tumultuous journey to entrepreneurship, showing that waiting for the perfect moment only keeps us stuck in an unfulfilled version of ourselves. If perfectionism has you paralyzed, this book will teach you that done beats perfect, and that confidence comes from action — not permission.

Mike Uttley, Small Business Consultant

Scary Good is a powerful and deeply human read. Angie shares her story with a level of honesty and clarity that pulls you right in — at times it felt like I was watching her life unfold moment by moment. Her writing is vivid and engaging, and I often felt as if I were walking beside her through some of the most challenging chapters of her journey.

The realness of this book moved me to tears more than once. Angie invites readers into both the strength and the struggle, creating something rare: a memoir filled with truth, purpose, insight, and hope. It's a reminder that alignment, healing, and growth are possible even in the hardest seasons. I am grateful for this book and cannot recommend it enough.

Jessica Visek, Career Coach and Founder of Your Career Partner

What a fantastic read. Angie shares her wild, adventurous life in a way that feels instantly relatable, whether you're deep in your career, building something new, or a mom rediscovering purpose after kids. She reminds us that humans still matter — and honestly, we all need that reminder in a world that feels more digital than ever.

Adrienne Kalivoda, Funeral Director at Kloecker Funeral Home and Crematory, Inc.

Angie shows that the Sunday Scaries should never hold us back — that we shouldn't be afraid to pause, reflect, and try something new. I read this book at a crossroads in my life, unsure of which path to take next, and it came at just the right time. This book gave me the motivation to take off the blinders and confidently take the next step. Thank you, Angie.

Katherine Anderson, Coach, Mentor, and Student Advocate

Life is an adventure, and *Scary Good* reminds me of that in the most honest and heartfelt way. The book offers courage to anyone facing a difficult moment and brings light to those standing at a crossroads. By the end, I found myself seeing the beauty and strength in an imperfect life — my own included. Even the messy parts hold something deeply meaningful and true.

Yun-Ya Yang, PhD

Angie Callen reminds us that we are all human — that every one of us experiences setbacks that shape our character and deepen our resilience. This book felt deeply personal to me because I've lived through so many of the moments she describes, and reading it brought me face-to-face with experiences I thought I had long processed. It also surfaced a familiar loneliness, the quiet question we all ask at some point: *Am I doing the right thing?*

To my surprise, reading about Angie's journey stirred emotions I didn't expect. When my sister asked what the book was about, I found myself in tears as I tried to explain it. *Scary Good* offers comfort and clarity, pairing practical advice with the reassurance that we are not alone in our struggles. Reading her words felt like receiving encouragement at exactly the moment I needed it.

Kathy Bailon, Founder of KB Career Coaching

Angie's story shows us that it's possible to get from one side of a deep canyon to the other if you just keep moving through it. Her journey is an inspiration for anyone who wants to make a big shift — those on the edge of one, those in the messy middle, and those who have already come out the other side. It might even reveal that you want something you didn't know you were allowed to want before.

Cary Rinken, Coach, Speaker, and Author

My attention was captured from the very first page. I couldn't wait to discover the next chapter of Angie's life and the powerful lessons woven through her stories. Her words challenge us to move beyond misalignment and the trap of being merely "fine," and instead pursue a life rich with meaning and purpose. *Scary Good* inspires us to iterate, refuse the status quo, and chase what truly aligns with who we are. This book will motivate, challenge, and empower you to identify what matters most — and confidently go after it.

Matthew Thomas, Career Strategist and Coach

Scary Good was exactly the boost I needed. Angie Callen's message — that the Sunday Scaries aren't a flaw but a signal — hit me in the best way. Her honest, energizing approach inspired me to start taking small, brave steps toward a life that feels aligned and exciting.

Zoe H., Fun Seeker and Amateur Mountain Biker

As someone whose career and confidence were shaped by Angie's coaching, I immediately recognized her voice in these pages — honest, grounding, and deeply compassionate. What resonated most was how she reframes the heaviness many of us feel on Sundays and turns it into something empowering. This book makes you feel understood, but more importantly, it gives you permission to rewrite the story behind that dread. Angie offers clarity, encouragement, and practical guidance in a way only she can. Anyone who's ever felt the Sunday Scaries will walk away feeling lighter and more hopeful.

Alicia Lomas, Founder and Principal of Lomas Manufacturing Consulting

Scary Good is a must-read. Angie's authenticity shines through from the first page. Her story normalizes life's ups and downs, and the messy middle we all shy away from openly talking about. I enjoyed following Angie's journey — watching her grow, find her community, and discover a true sense of belonging. She's truly an inspiration for all.

Kristen Stewart, Career Coach and Founder of Careers Align, Normalizing Career Breaks

Scary Good is exactly what its title promises — insightful, energizing, and refreshingly human. Angie Callen offers life lessons delivered with infectious enthusiasm, blending memoir, motivation, and the core tenets of her career-coaching philosophy. While chronicling a journey not many of us have lived — business flops, housing challenges, tiny living, and plenty of scraped knees — she offers every reader a mirror in which they'll see themselves. Through humor, honesty, and deeply relatable self-reflection, Angie shows what it takes to reject misalignment and pursue a life built on values, intention, and authenticity. It's not neat or linear, but it is possible — and profoundly inspiring.

Laurel Tesoro, Roaring Fork CrossFit Owner, Mountain Biker, and Recovering Perfectionist

Angie Callen knocks it out of the park with this memoir that is simultaneously introspective, inspiring, and entertaining. Her story demonstrates the magic that happens when we stop trying to compartmentalize ourselves into a "professional persona" and a "regular life persona," and instead choose to be our whole, messy, inspiring selves.

Diana Alt, No BS Career Coach and Host of the *Work Should Feel Good* Podcast

If you're a recovering pragmatist who wants to play it safe in your career yet still feel truly alive each day, you need to read this book. *Scary Good* should come with a warning label: if I were still working in some of my past jobs, it would probably have talked me into quitting. *Scary Good* isn't just a manual for what to do next if you don't like your job, feel fine but not fulfilled, or sense that something is missing. It's a personal story filled with inspiration and nuggets of wisdom that will appeal to a wide audience. You may see yourself in these pages as you consider what it means to live fully, day in and day out.

Kelcie Stone

In *Scary Good*, Angie Callen writes with brave, raw honesty about the personal and professional sides of work, risk, and reinvention. The result is a clarifying and motivating lens for anyone navigating their next professional chapter.

Joy Hamilton, PhD

Scary Good is the kind of book that makes you feel seen in all the best and hardest ways. Angie blends honesty, humor, and lived wisdom into stories that remind us we're allowed to question our path, reinvent ourselves, and choose a life that actually fits. Her candor is refreshing, her insights are grounding, and her ability to turn messy moments into meaningful lessons is a true gift. It's the kind of book you dog-ear, highlight, and return to whenever you need a nudge forward.

Denise Bitler, Award-Winning Résumé Writer, Executive Career Coach, and Nationally Recognized Thought Leader and Speaker

Scary Good is the type of coaching book that doesn't assume everything you've ever known or done was a failure. It's not peachy or pretentious. Instead, it celebrates the beauty of the journey, the joy in the struggles, and the rewards that come from taking action. Through real-world examples of the messy bits of life, Angie presents practical methods that help readers persevere and build the life they want.

Jessica Stott, Project Manager

Angie Callen's sense of humor, timing, and irony make this leadership memoir a delight to read. Follow her through adventures in accidental and on-purpose living, and gain insights into polishing your own leadership potential. You'll love her style, her joy, and her guidance.

Debra O'Reilly, Founder of ResumeWriter.com

Scary Good is a fun, adventurous, and inspiring story about daring to go against the grain of what society calls "success" and creating a life on your own terms. Angie's willingness to put herself out there, trust the process, and keep moving forward makes this book relatable, energizing, and impossible to put down. Her voice jumps off the page, and the lessons she shares remind us that self-help doesn't have to feel heavy — it can be bold, human, and even fun. This is a story you can read in an afternoon and walk away changed.

F.J. Carleo, Men's Life Coach and Founder of Built to Elevate

Scary Good is so engaging — Angie's humility and humor make every story land, and the narrative arc pulls you in immediately. Her voice is so thoroughly authentic it feels like you're hearing her read it aloud, and little bits of her heart are on every page. Even with such a conversational tone, the writing is tight and compelling. As she does in person, Angie inspires without a hint of didacticism or superiority.

Lili Foggle, Interview Coach and Founder of Impressive Interviewing

Scary Good is a breath of fresh air. Angie Callen writes with such candor and warmth that it feels like sitting down with her over coffee — encouraging, honest, and surprisingly funny. Her storytelling pulled me in immediately, and I found myself abandoning my usual editor's instinct because I was so invested in the narrative. Angie's ability to help others navigate difficult chapters comes through on every page, and her resilience makes this book both relatable and uplifting.

Andrew Altenburg, Events Manager and Cartoonist

Reading *Scary Good* feels like talking with an old friend about life's challenges and figuring out how to tackle them together. Between moments of laughing out loud and quiet introspection, the book offers sage life advice for people at any stage — along with a few great quips along the way. If you're anything like me, you won't be able to put it down, and you may even find inspiration for your own Scary Good life.

Ryan Donohue, Senior Executive in the Nonprofit Sector

Scary GOOD

A BOOK FOR THE BURNT OUT, THE BRAVE, AND AND EVERYONE IN BETWEEN

ANGIE CALLEN

Scary

GOOD

DISCOVERING LIFE BEYOND
the Sunday Scaries

THE
MODERN
COACH
PRESS
Glenwood Springs, CO

Scary Good: Discovering Life Beyond the Sunday Scaries
© 2026 by Angie Callen

THE
MODERN
COACH
PRESS
Glenwood Springs, CO

The Modern Coach Press
P.O. Box 152
Glenwood Springs, CO 81601

Publisher's Note:
This publication is designed to provide accurate and authoritative information in regard to the subject matter covered. It is sold with the understanding that neither the author nor the publisher is engaged in rendering legal, investment, accounting, or other professional services. While the publisher and author have used their best efforts in preparing this book, they make no representations or warranties with respect to the accuracy or completeness of the contents and specifically disclaim any implied warranties of merchantability or fitness for a particular purpose. The advice and strategies contained herein may not be suitable for your situation. You should consult with a professional when appropriate. Neither the publisher nor the author shall be liable for any loss of profit or any other commercial damages, including but not limited to special, incidental, consequential, personal, or other damages.

Scary Good: Discovering Life Beyond the Sunday Scaries — 1st ed.
Paperback: 979-8-9942136-0-5
Hardback: ISBN: 979-8-9942136-1-2
Ebook: ISBN: 979-8-9942136-2-9

Editorial Development: Kathy Sparrow, The Literary Midwife
Book Design: George Stevens, G Sharp Design, LLC

Printed in the United States of America

For Jim, who has weathered every chapter of this book with me — save the first. Considering many of the events, both included and conveniently left out, that's no small feat. Without you, *Combating the Sunday Scaries* would be a lot more boring, and life would be a lot less adventureful. Also, my author name would be completely different.

Love you.

Table of Contents

Foreword

by Justin Schenck

THE FIRST TIME I met Angie Callen, it took about twenty seconds to realize we were cut from the same cloth. Two sides of Pennsylvania, same wavelength. We were both speakers in the same circle, both podcasters who love real conversation, and both obsessed with one question: _How do we help good humans live more meaningful lives?_

We've both been there…broke, burnt out, and wondering what's next. Rock bottoms that test your faith, your identity, and your ability to get back up again. I've had mine. Angie's had hers. And what I love most about this book is that she doesn't just tell you how to climb out; she _shows_ you how to find the meaning in the climb itself.

Angie and I joke that success is 80 percent mindset, 20 percent everything else, but there's truth there. Your skills, plans, and strategies mean nothing if your head and heart aren't aligned, and that alignment doesn't happen by accident. _Scary Good_ pulls back the curtain on that process, offering an important reminder that your mess can become your message if you're willing to get honest about it.

As I read these pages, I kept nodding. She talks about purpose, about doing the inner work, about staying humble enough to keep learning, all themes that have shaped my journey. When I hit my own low point after losing my mom to a twenty-year battle with opioids, I learned a truth that Angie writes about beautifully: you can't help others if you don't take care of yourself first. You must first fill your cup, and what overflows is for everyone else. This is the only way to serve others at a high level for a long time.

There's a line in this book that hits hard: *"Humans are, by nature, inquisitive creatures."* We're wired to ask questions, to seek, to move before we're ready. Look, I'm a big believer that curiosity is a superpower. That curiosity, that willingness to ask the right questions and then begin anyway, is what Angie captures so well. It's what drives every entrepreneur, every leader, every human who's ever dared to want something better.

What I admire about Angie is that she doesn't preach from the mountaintop, even when she's literally on a mountaintop. She's right there in the mud with you…laughing, learning, and telling it like it is. She'll make you laugh, nod, and probably see a bit of yourself in her stories about life, leadership, and what it really means to build something bigger than yourself.

Scary Good isn't a book you'll read once and shelve. It's one you'll dog-ear, highlight, and come back to when you forget who you are or why you started. It's an invitation to slow down, to trust yourself, and to design a life that feels as good on the inside as it looks from the outside.

If you've picked up this book, you're already doing the hardest part — showing up for yourself.

Angie's just here to remind you that you already have what it takes.

Because at the end of the day, the *Scary Good* life isn't about never falling down. It's about finding the courage to rise, again and again, and realizing you were capable all along.

Justin Schenck

Host, *Growth Now Movement* Podcast
Creator, *Growth Now Summit Live*

The average American experiences the Sunday Scaries 36 times a year.

Sunday Scaries /ˈsən-ˌdā ˈsker-ēz/ *noun*

Temporary anxiety experienced by humans at the end of the weekend, triggered by the thought of the workweek ahead. See also: letting Monday ruin your Sunday.   *Talker Research for Pacific Foods*

Author's Note

WHEN I FIRST began writing weekly *Sunday Scaries* newsletters in April of 2022, I had no idea where it would lead. It certainly wasn't here. I was just trying to make sense of life — the messy, the hopeful, and the in-between — while helping others do the same. Yet somewhere along my journey to rebuild after rock bottom, I created something bigger than myself.

I realized what I'd really been documenting wasn't business or career growth.

It was being human.

Every story, every lesson, every "Scary Good" moment shapes who we are and how we live out our purpose in the world — which is why we can never forget that humans still matter, and that starts with ourselves.

Scary Good is a collection of stories, reflections, and reminders that, regardless of how chaotic life gets, we always have a choice: **to design our lives instead of living by default**. To reconnect to what matters. To keep moving. To find our purpose — one Sunday, one story, one small act of courage at a time.

If you've ever felt stuck in the space between who you are and who you're meant to be, this book is for you. I hope these stories, and accompanying teachings, help you feel seen, understood, a little less lonely, and a little more confident that you have everything you need to build the career, business, and life you deserve.

So grab a cup of coffee and settle in.

Inside you'll find honest (and sometimes uncomfortable) experiences that prove growth is rarely linear, bite-sized insights pulled straight from the newsletter that started it all, and conversational companions in the form of *No More Mondays* podcast pairings.

Think of this as part memoir, part field guide, part conversation with a friend who tells it like it is. Take what you need, leave the rest, and let these pages remind you that courage, confidence, and community are all part of being human.

And at the end of the day, whatever you do…

Don't let Mondays ruin your Sundays.

Chapter 1

LIFESTYLES OF THE OVERWORKED AND ANXIOUS

Champagne Wishes and Sewer Line Dreams

"Only I can change my life. No one can do it for me."

Carol Burnett

I'M A RECOVERING engineer who loves people.

That one sentence alone should tell you I was destined for the Sunday Scaries the minute I enrolled in Civil Engineering at Carnegie Mellon. It just took about ten years to get there.

Dread for the work week really hit circa 2009, shortly after my big move from Boston to Breckenridge, in the heart of the Colorado Rockies. Every Sunday afternoon, I'd make the mental move from the euphoria of mountain play to the anxiety about the start of the week. Yet each Monday Morning, I dutifully showed up to my cubicle straight out of *Office Space*, peering through a screensaver-like window at the most incredible sapphire blue sky, as the outdoors seemingly mocked me: Look at what you could have...*back to drawing sewer lines*.

On paper, I had it made: a steady paycheck, a stable engineering job, a company willing to relocate me across the country, and an apartment across from the ski lift. I was the most gainfully employed ski bum you'd ever meet (there's a great LinkedIn job title), and every minute spent in that cubicle working on the equivalent of TPS reports made me long to be a gainfully *unemployed* ski bum more and more.

Don't get me wrong — moving to Colorado was awesome, and I have my engineering career to thank for that. But it was also the wake-up call that showed me just how wrong engineering was for me (and, frankly, how wrong I was for it). As if dying a slow death by detailed minutiae weren't enough, it turns out I wasn't so jazzed about paving paradise to put up a parking lot.

For someone who thrives on impact and connection, showing up to a sterile cubicle to design paved parking on National Forest land so ski resorts could pack in more cars was...soul-crushing. My work in Boston had largely involved brownfield sites and redevelopment projects where construction was actually an improvement. Now? I was destroying Bambi's woods, and that was more disheartening than a post-vacation inbox.

As if the mountains themselves weren't changing my perspective on life, the nature of the work (or should I say the *anti-nature* of the work) was starting to shift how I saw the vocation I'd chosen, and that was unsettling. The signs were starting to add up.

I wasn't just suffering from the Sunday Scaries; I was suffocating in a career that wasn't *me*.

The change in setting made the mismatch as painfully obvious as it should have been during my naps in freshman-year physics. My dread for those lectures really should have been a clear indication that I was barking up the wrong tree. If I'm honest, I knew somewhere around my junior year that I didn't want to be an engineer, but when you're self-funding your Carnegie Mellon tuition, you don't switch majors three-quarters of the way through.

Truth be told, I didn't go into engineering because I had some burning passion for infrastructure or stormwater design. I chose it because, as a high school senior, I had no idea what I wanted to do with my life — and that felt like a dirty little secret for a top performer. I was self-conscious about my inability to connect to a college major because it made me feel less intelligent than I knew I was, but looking back, it makes sense.

They don't teach entrepreneurship in Podunkville, Pennsylvania.

My dad, who also happened to be my high school math teacher (for three years), suggested the idea to me. I can hear it plain as day: "Ang, you're good at math and science, why don't you be an engineer?"

As an approval-seeking seventeen-year-old who respected my dad's opinion, had zero interest in disappointing him, and had no better idea of my own, I took the advice. I researched the options and chose civil engineering over other disciplines...

May 18, 2025

22 Years, 1 Hard Hat, and 0 Sunday Scaries Later

The civil engineering grads at CMU wear hard hats to commencement, complete with a tassel taped to the top! Talk about funny looks...

That one detail would end up being a metaphor for my life and career, where I've never been one to follow the norm, and it all started with a people-lover who didn't fit in as an engineer.

I was "doomed" from the start...and for that, I'm grateful.

💡 Lesson: The best things happen when you stop trying to blend in and start being you.

because it was the one where you supposedly got to talk to people the most.

Tip from your coach: If "How much will I get to talk to people?" is your top decision-making parameter for a career path, engineering might not be your calling.

Regardless, I stuck it out, earned the degree, moved to Boston, and started climbing the ladder.

Turns out, being an engineer who loves people has its perks.

Two years into my career, which started at an internationally acclaimed landscape architecture firm, I moved to a more traditional, albeit still global, engineering company to work on what was, at the time, the biggest project for their largest client, Lowe's Home Improvement Warehouse. They were in the throes of a major Northeast expansion, and I landed a spot on the crown jewel of projects: the store projected to be the highest-grossing location in the country.

I was hired as a junior engineer in a support role, but things escalated quickly when the lead engineer I reported to left the company. Thus, the "Angie can do it" mantra that would follow me through the rest of my career was born. It was flattering at first — being seen as *the fixer* — until I realized "Angie can do it" really meant "Angie *will* do it," and that perpetuated a vicious cycle. The harder I worked, the more addicted I became to being indispensable.

At twenty-five, three years into a career designing pipes to make shit flow downhill, I became the second most important person on a behemoth of a project in one of the hardest permitting districts in America. As if that weren't enough, the department vice president and client lead resigned a few months later.

Strike that. *Most important person.*

There I was: the youngest one in the room, a twenty-something woman in a male-dominated industry, telling everyone else what to do. Before I knew it, I was presenting at town council meetings, negotiating with zoning boards until 2 a.m., and flying to Lowe's corporate headquarters to sit in on design meetings with executives twice my age.

Everyone was mistaking control for competence, including me. I was trying to keep up the charade, overwhelmed by the sheer volume of work and lack of experience, all while describing site plans and defending stormwater designs I barely had time to understand. Somewhere in Pittsburgh, my physics professor laughed.

But don't worry, Angie will save the day.

Along with more responsibility than any twenty-something should be expected to take on came some fringe "perks" — as some would call them.

I guess that's what happens when you're the rare engineer who can talk to people.

Case in point: the company golf tournament. A few days before the event, our CEO tore his Achilles tendon, and guess who was *voluntold* to take his place on the team with Lowe's execs?

Relevant note: I've golfed four times in my life. This was lucky number three.

My injured boss was having the time of his life driving the drink cart (*if the CEO wants to drive the drink cart at the company golf tournament, the CEO drives the drink cart)* while I schmoozed my way through eighteen holes, and somehow won a bottle of Dom Pérignon. *Closest to the pin* is quite the accomplishment when you're competing against a whopping two other women in the tourney.

From the outside, I looked like the perfect fast-tracking young professional. On the inside, I was barely holding it together.

You know what I'm talking about (and you don't have to be redlining plans at midnight to get it). Maybe it's managing a classroom, an unrealistic sales goal, or the insurmountable load at home; we all have some version of "in over your head but smiling your way through it anyway."

I was the poster child for grin and bear it.

Between the long hours, harassment on job sites, and the paycheck I knew was lower than that of less-qualified male peers, my life looked less like "overnight success" and more like a construction site where the work never stopped, and I was the only one holding the shovel.

Snowboarding was my one release. I'd taken "to the hill" during my first winter after moving to Boston and was instantly hooked (I guess I could have picked up more harmful coping mechanisms, eh?). I loved sneaking away from what seemed like 9-9-6[1] work expectations to night ski at Wachusett and then hit Vermont, New Hampshire, and Maine on weekends.

---

1 9-9-6: working 9 a.m. to 9 p.m., six days a week. Productivity culture at its best.

But after one trip to Colorado in 2007, it was game over. Why drive I-95 to ski frozen boilerplate[2] in Maine when I could live in the powder-filled Rockies?

So, that's what I did.

When the opportunity to transfer west opened in 2008, I jumped. New adventure. Bigger mountains. Better skiing. A chance to keep building my career in a new setting.

I signed the paperwork, hired a moving van, packed my life (along with that of the long-term relationship who came with me), and we moved across the country.

While I'd love to tell you fun road-trip stories about seeing the world's largest ball of twine on what *should* have been my first cross-country road trip, this relocation was less adventure and more airport. A JetBlue flight (pre-Wi-Fi, of course), a car shipped 2,000 miles, and one drugged-up cat who fit entirely under the seat in front of me — no playlists, no open road, just a one-way ticket to 9,757 feet above sea level.

I started work in Breckenridge on September 8, 2008. Seven days later, Lehman Brothers collapsed, the economy imploded, and all the high-profile projects I thought I was moving west to lead disappeared overnight. *Great timing, Ang.*

Instead of rubbing elbows with bigwigs and managing flashy flagship projects, I was parked in a cubicle, with the mind-numbing task of redlining CAD drawings, staring out the window at the mountains while little pieces of myself died

2 "Boilerplate": affectionate New England slang for rock-hard, icy "snow" — a.k.a. "the Ice Coast."

with every passing Monday. The engineer who loves people didn't stand out in this dwindling crowd.

At this point, you may expect a quick resolution to this messy series of events: I stuck it out, the industry improved, and I climbed the ranks until I finally left to start my own business.

Oh, no no no. There were still a lot of hard lessons to learn before I figured out what alignment actually looks like.

In other words: We still have a lot of book to go.

Life has a funny way of forcing us to surrender before we're ready, doesn't it? Sometimes the bottom has to drop out to get our attention. That version for you may not have included the global economic crisis that was the 2008 crash, but I bet you know the feeling: the promotion falls through, the pink slip gets slid across the table, or the plan you've been banking on (pun intended) evaporates overnight.

It wouldn't be the last time life pulled the rug out from under me, but in this particular case, it was entirely out of my control. So, I did what a lot of people do when they're fighting reality: I disconnected. I skied at lunch, although to be fair, that's what most folks in these parts do to cope with stress. I took furlough days to chase powder in Beaver Creek[3].

I soaked up every bit of joy I could find outside the office, because nothing inside those walls provided it, while telling myself I was doing the responsible thing — doing what any successful adult should do: staying the course. Keep the job. Micromanage the misery. Accept the mediocrity.

---

3 Let's be real: the actual reason I played hooky was to enjoy the warm, fresh-baked cookies they hand out at Base Village at 3:30 p.m. Free. Cookies.

I wasn't seeking a solution; I was settling for survival.

Admitting I needed a change was a harder pill to swallow than any late-night submittal deadline. Quitting a prestigious job isn't what valedictorians and logical people do, and leaving my chosen career field felt even more outrageous, given my upbringing.

Growing up in a traditional Baby Boomer household, "stability" was the gold standard. While my parents made me feel as if I could be anything I wanted to be, I'm pretty sure "anything" meant one of the five respectable careers of the nineties: doctor, lawyer, engineer, accountant, teacher.

And there I was with one of them. A $150,000 degree, the student loans to prove it, and the associated career that had just delivered me 2,000 miles away from everything I knew. How could I admit I had picked the wrong path? Made a bad move? Tell my proud family I was ready to walk away from the career I had worked so hard (and gone into so much debt) to build?

I also had to admit it to myself.

Talk about a hard confession. Once we say something out loud, even to ourselves, we can't unhear it. I didn't have the language for burnout, misalignment, or the Sunday Scaries yet, but I did know something had to give.

It certainly wasn't going to be the mountains.

From that point forward, the only thing I had left to do was face the truth and decide where to go. Control had been my coping mechanism, but it was time to take the first real act of courage. It was time to let go.

Sometimes, surrender is what makes space for possibility.

When we start to let go of assumptions, ditch societal norms, and question the expectations placed on us by others, life doesn't just get interesting. It gets honest. And unpredictable. In the best possible way.

We expect things to get messier, and they do (ask me how I know), but here's the paradox: in loosening our grip on the control we think we have but never will, we also let go of a little of the perfectionist chokehold. We stop managing our lives like projects and start living them like the experiences we're meant to have.

The possibilities most certainly won't be ideal, and the outcome won't look like that vision board you spent an entire Saturday assembling from magazine cut-outs and Elmer's glue. But you never know what kind of clarity will come from a Craigslist job in a mountain town that barely covers rent but lays the groundwork to an entirely different life.

My first career change (more on this later) wasn't particularly smart, and it was by no means graceful, but it was mine, and for the first time in my adult life…

*I felt like **me**.*

If Sunday Scaries had a root cause, it wouldn't be stress or even the sheer volume of things on our plates. It would be misalignment. The slow deterioration of living a life that looks right on paper but feels wrong in practice. Holding on to careers, titles, or roles that drain our energy while we simultaneously fight to let go. Keeping up appearances day after day, week after week, until that recurring Sunday dread starts showing up like clockwork.

But we do it. We cope. We keep on keepin' on.

We hit the desk on Monday morning, pretending everything is four-letter-F-word F.I.N.E., fine. We try to hold it all together. Grip tighter. Look more polished, thinking, "if I can just get ahead, I'll be saved."

Alignment and purpose don't work that way, but there we stand, holding on to the *illusion* of control…sweaty palms and all.

Control is a coping mechanism. Perfection is performative. Overwhelm becomes the norm. Before we know it, we've burned ourselves out attempting to uphold a handed-down belief system and maintain someone else's version of success.

We drown ourselves in distractions, the busyness badge, and over-the-top expectations for work, relationships, life — all of it, to subdue that nagging feeling that there's more. And then… we just keep piling it on! Overcommitted schedules, over-the-top standards, endless yeses, because stopping might mean confronting the truth: we're overwhelmed, we're exhausted, and we're not living the life we want.

There's a Japanese concept called ikigai, which combines "iki" (life) and "gai" (value), meaning that which makes life worth living.

The visual is similar to what we Westerners call a fancy Venn diagram, but the point is to find the intersection of what you love, are good at, the world needs, and gives you meaning.

💡 Lesson: Success isn't about doing more; it's about doing what matters most.

If you've ever stood in the kitchen on a Sunday night, staring blankly into the fridge while your brain loads every single open tab on Monday's to-do list, you're not alone.

According to the American Psychological Association, nearly **one in four adults**[4] feel so stressed they cannot function. And one in three adults feels overwhelmed by their stress. That's only going to get worse as the world gets even louder, faster, and more demanding.

We think doing more will somehow give us peace, but when we try to be everything to everyone else, we end up being nothing to ourselves. Perfection is not sustainable in the long term, nor is control. Neither is a cure for the overwhelming level of responsibility we've placed on ourselves, and none of it will bring alignment. Ultimately, all we're doing is disappointing ourselves more than anyone else. I can't think of a worse fate than to think back one day and say, "I should have done more for myself."

Clarity, confidence, and contentment take us much further in this world than keeping up with the Joneses or living under someone else's definition of success ever will. But doing more will never get us there. Alignment comes from knowing who we are, what we value, and what actually ***matters to us.***

Not only do most of us never stop *doing* long enough to define success for ourselves, even if we do, we set it aside for someone else's checklist. From the pressure to have a social-media-worthy vacation to the fear of failing, we stay stuck, and we stay small.

---

4 *Stress in America 2022 Report*. American Psychological Association. In other words, we're all one push notification away from a full-systems shutdown. Or a therapy appointment.

March 22, 2024

Are You the Hero of Your Sunday Scaries Story?

Know What Success Means to You

It's easy to get caught up in what the world tells us success looks like instead of defining it for ourselves and allowing that to translate into our unique life goals and vision.

Consider your values, passions, maybe even go crazy and think about those dreams you believe can't come true because society says so. You'll be surprised at what's possible!

Lesson: Push the envelope and define success on your terms.

But here's a hard truth to kick off this book:

Fear kills more dreams than failure ever will.

We live in a society that rewards picture-perfect and fears failure, probably more than at any other point in history thus far. Not convinced? Just think about how afraid we are to look our age! Perfection doesn't make us strong; it makes us brittle. Control doesn't bring peace; it robs us of it. We end up living on the edge of a stress explosion while churning highlight reels into Instagram feeds, hoping *likes* will prove we've got it made.

But controlling every detail and making everyone else see how tidy our lives are will never rid us of the Sunday Scaries. I mean, when was the last time civilization collapsed because someone loaded the dishwasher the wrong way (*don't ask my husband that question*)?

Acceptance. Authenticity. ***Knowing***. That's where the magic is, and that's why the bravest thing we can often do on a Sunday when the world is spinning out of control is stop.

Stop trying to solve next week.
Stop trying to prove you've got it all together.
Stop trying to win the week before it even begins.
Stop trying to be perfect when being present will do just fine.
And for crying out loud, stop reloading the dishwasher.

Overwhelm thrives in vagueness, which is why half our Sunday night is spent color-coding a calendar that's blown up by 11 a.m. on Monday. Everything is urgent. Everything is important. Everything must be done perfectly. And at an A+ level. I'm exhausted just typing that.

How about being honest with ourselves? That'll bring some clarity, and the good news is we don't have to do more to get there. We can interrupt the cycle. We can choose alignment over anxiety, presence over performance, and progress over perfection.

You don't need to impress your way into a meaningful life.

The world will always ask for more.
Your life begins when you stop giving it.

Let this be your start.

No More Mondays Companion Episodes

Embracing Imperfection: How to Overcome the Pitfalls of Perfectionism with Dr. Greg Chasson *(December 3, 2025)*

Struggling with Imposter Syndrome? Learn how to Overcome the Imposter with Kris Kelso *(December 6, 2023)*

Stop the Proving, Pleasing, and Perfecting with Heather Whelpley *(October 12, 2022)*

Chapter 2

SOUL-SEARCHING AND SUBARUS

The Truth About Transitions

"The mountains are calling, and I must go."

John Muir

THE MOVE TO Breckenridge wasn't a leap of faith; it was a dream that wouldn't go away. A call I couldn't ignore. If I had stayed in Boston, I knew I would have regretted it for the rest of my life, and the boyfriend in tow knew that, too.

For a while, it was great. Angie's honeymoon with Colorado. Midweek lunch breaks on the slopes, sunny weekends summiting peaks, the kind of crisp blue-sky mornings that make you think you've died and gone to heaven.

I was sure I had.

However, within weeks — no *days* — of my arrival, the honeymoon ended. The economy tanked, projects disappeared, and my step up became a step back. Any redeeming qualities of engineering, few as they already were, were quickly fading.

Things on the home front weren't any better. The "we" who had moved across the country together essentially became roommates: two people living under the same roof but wanting different things. Our life goals were quickly diverging, or to be fair, mine were in upheaval while his remained the same, and that wasn't something we could overcome. Nine months after we arrived, he left.

It wasn't dramatic or messy, but it still sucked. One of the last few things anchoring me to the "before days" was just another layer being stripped away from the life I once knew. The dream scenario was getting a little cloudy, and while so much of it still felt right, it also didn't exactly feel stable. The apartment on French Street, across from the ski hill, was suddenly too big, too quiet, and too expensive. Career aspirations had been reduced to an internship-level of responsibility, and I'm pretty sure even the cat was lonely.

You know what's weird? Even while everything around me felt like an amorphous blob of uncertainty and change, I was experiencing…*a knowing*. I would never have been able to explain that or even identify it at the time, but my intuition told me I was where I was meant to be.

That sure as heck didn't come without a fair share of challenges. I was suddenly alone and completely independent in a remote, expensive ski town, with every single possibility in front of me. Did I have a clue how to tap into those possibilities?

Nope. Only the willingness to do so. *I know I can figure it out. I want to figure it out. I **have to** figure it out.*

I got scrappy (let's hear it for grit!). Mandatory weekly furlough days meant less money but more skiing. I put my student loans into forbearance and traded the cute little apartment on French Street for a share in a townhouse just outside town.

The only car we had headed back East with the other half, so I shelled out $4,000 for a 2001 Subaru Impreza with a muffler that let anyone know I was coming from four blocks away, and had so much rust on the hood, it looked like it had been through war.

My friends called it the go-kart — the embodiment of a (un)gainfully employed ski bum who probably had less money in the bank than the *actual* ski bums, save the 401(k) we don't talk about today…RIP.

Cash drifted in and out of my life faster than the snow. I spent my money on ski passes, camping gear, and a tent; true signs that I was becoming a mountain girl. (The latter I'm proud to say I still have today: my husband, Jim, jokes that the back-packing tent was part of my dowry, along with the aforementioned cat, Jax, also RIP).

As a college grad who never took the token backpacking trip to Europe and started my professional career two weeks after graduation, it felt like I was finally experiencing my "gap year." (*When did that even become a thing!?!*). Despite having a relatively solid paycheck and great health insurance, I was the happiest,

June 4, 2023

Wish Your Sunday Scaries Good Luck

Time in the outdoors is proven to boost your mood and provide a welcome distraction from technology and other stimuli that can make it hard to focus on yourself, what you want in life, and where you're headed.

💡 Lesson: Get outside and reflect on what's most important to you.

poorest, most out-of-control, twenty-eight-year-old people-loving engineer you had ever met.

I was living.

Fancy Pass in the Holy Cross Wilderness circa 2009.

Sure, there were days when I felt 100 percent untethered, resigned to the fact that I wasn't going to be able to "make it work." But my gut told me I was onto something, and I followed that intuition. Regardless of the struggles, the loneliness, the seeking, and the identity crisis, that deep-down **knowing** is what carried me through the looming transition. It's what gave me the grit to keep going and the strength to believe it was going to work out...*somehow*.

Packing up the house on French Street marked the first time I truly understood why things often have to crumble before they can be rebuilt. Not only was the last piece of the "us" who had moved across the country falling away, but with it went the very last shred of that girl who had arrived with it.

This was the first of the multiple rock bottoms I'd face as an adult, but like most of them, it came with an unexpected sense of relief. Possibilities. Hope. Leaving that creaky-floored place on French Street, charming as it was, was more cathartic than crisis.

I had fought so hard to get here, to literally reach this mountain town I'd dreamed of living in, but the reality didn't look anything like I had pictured. I was trading postcard perfection for raw guts, and if you know anything about me, you know that's exactly where the real Angie began to emerge.

My definition of success was starting to shift. I no longer needed the big-eyed reaction when I told some dude in a bar I was a civil engineer. I didn't need a car sans rust or a climb up the corporate ladder I had always assumed I'd ascend. I was starting to decide what I wanted in life — not just in Colorado or in Breckenridge, but for my overall existence. I was no longer bound by familial expectations, the rat race of a city, or the wishes of the "we" who arrived together.

For the first time, the only voice I had to listen to was my own.

But, of course, that doesn't mean I actually listened to that voice. There was still part of me fighting to control the instability and uncertainty, trying to ignore the intuition telling me it was time for (another) change. So, I did what many of us do when we're terrified by the thoughts in our heads and the sound of our own voice: I worked harder. I stayed busy. I got trigger-happy on the "apply button" for every random job in a mountain town.

I tried to look (and feel) like I was fine.

I kept skiing at lunch to prove — to myself and everyone else — that mountain life was everything I'd dreamed. Even though I was working a reduced schedule, I showed up to work early, smiled through meetings, and acted like drafting eight hours a day wasn't slowly draining my soul.

I went out with friends, enjoyed too many shots of Tuaca on more occasions than I'd like to admit, and posted Facebook photos of perfect bluebird days to convince my family back East that everything was great.

Because admitting the truth — that I was lost, scared, and unsure of what came next — felt humiliating. I kept up the façade, attempting to ignore the multiplying losses around me while quietly wondering if *I was the failure*.

I know now that those failures weren't endings. They were opportunities. Invitations. A reset button. The beginning of something new.

Like most beginnings, it didn't arrive neatly packaged with step-by-step instructions. Mine showed up with more uncertainty than a weather forecast in the Rockies — and a gut feeling that something had to change.

And I was the only one around to do anything about it.

*When change knocks, we can either answer...
or it'll let itself in.*

While we hate how it feels at the time, transitions don't really strip things away from us. They reveal what's waiting beneath. Yes, that process may remove the things we *thought* defined us — relationships, job titles, the car, the cute house, the golden handcuffs — but once all that surface-level stuff is set aside, we're left with some amazing raw material. That's what we're meant to build from.

Labels are easy; facing who we are without them is the hard part.

If Chapter One was about a wake-up call to misalignment, Chapter Two is where the work begins; it's where we start breaking down what was and evaluating inherited beliefs, so we can begin the slow process of becoming who we're meant to be.

We get to (yes, *get* to!) explore what's on the inside — what we value, how we treat people, what fires us up, and maybe most importantly: *what is our purpose?*

The tricky thing about this part of the transition?

There's no "how-to" guide.

There's no "Welcome to the Hamster Wheel!" pamphlet handed to us when the plan falls apart, and we're stuck in limbo. Instead, we're given questions, uncertainty, and the feeling that we may have just lost our minds.

September 21, 2025

Give Your Sunday Scaries a Performance Review

Nothing is meant to go at 100 percent 100 percent of the time, which means gaps of all sorts are natural and necessary. Rest, recovery, sabbaticals, stillness; this is what makes our stories sustainable.

Lesson: Where can you create a little space for yourself this week?

Maybe we did. And maybe that's exactly what's supposed to happen.

The irony is that transitions ask us to pause. To stop. To wait. And in that waiting, we're forced to reflect, and maybe for the first time, feel the feelings that we really hate feeling (yes, you read that correctly). It is those very emotions that not only force us to admit what we've been avoiding, but also allow us to create space for what's to come. That just never happens as fast as we think it should.

Change always takes longer than we want it to.

A shift in seasons doesn't just change our circumstances; it changes *us*. It helps us shed what no longer serves us and challenges us to ask and answer questions we wouldn't necessarily face. It requires grieving what *was* to build readiness for what *could be*.

This is precisely why we feel like failures during transitions. But…

A person cannot be a failure.

Failure is an instance, not an identity, and that's why transitions, as messy as they are, are also where we start to learn, grow, and *come home to ourselves*.

If the root cause of Sunday dread is misalignment, then transitions are where that misalignment comes to light. They're the spotlight that says, *Hey, something here isn't working anymore.*

The problem? We hate this part. We want clarity without the chaos. We want to skip to the ending without wading through the middle, even though that's exactly where we have to be for the transformation to happen. This is why people start new jobs and still feel dread at 4:30 p.m. on Sunday. It's why we move to new cities and still feel lost. It's why we check all the boxes and still feel like something's missing.

We can't outrun the need for transition, big or small. No matter how much we wish that one particular bag would get lost on the flight from Denver to Pittsburgh, it'll follow us around until we unpack it.

According to psychologist Bruce Feiler, all meaningful life changes include a holding pattern with three phases: *the long goodbye, the messy middle, and the new beginning.*[5] Most of us underestimate how long that middle takes to pass. It is critical to grieve what was and question what could be to take a step toward what's next.

So here's what I want you to know:

You are allowed to not have it figured out yet.
You are allowed to outgrow what once fit perfectly.
You are allowed to take a step forward without knowing the path you're on.
You are allowed to change your mind.
You are allowed to explore.

---

5 "Handling Life Transitions: Interview with Bruce Feiler," *Nir and Far*, 2022. https://www.nirandfar.com/life-transitions-bruce-feiler/ Translation: basically, life's one long layover, and we're stuck in boarding group 86 with no gate updates.

Sunday Scaries (and the anxiety, depression, sadness, etc., etc., they represent) feed on uncertainty and the fear of the in-between. They convince us we've failed, we're behind, we should be doing, looking, feeling better, and that we have no other choice but to accept the status quo.

The irony of that is that the in-between isn't where we fail; it's where we *find* ourselves.

Whether your messy middle has already come and gone, or it has yet to arrive, know this: it won't last forever. Even when it feels like you've been running in circles and waiting for that moment for an eternity, keep going.

You're not stuck.
You're just in the *process*.
The process of becoming.
You are not your job. You are not the relationship that ended.
You are not the plan that fell apart.
You are the person who is brave enough to keep going anyway.

The Sunday Scaries don't stand a chance against someone willing to stand in the messy middle.

No More Mondays Companion Episodes

The Quest for Happiness: How to Find Meaning in Our Fast-Paced World with Ashish Kothari *(July 26, 2023)*

Walking in Purpose: How to Live and Grow in Alignment with Your Strengths with John Thompson, III *(March 22, 2023)*

How to Thrive in a Rapidly Changing World with John Saunders *(October 13, 2021)*

Chapter 3

PERMISSION TO BE GRATEFUL

And Other Radical Acts of Rebellion

"Life changes very quickly, in a very
positive way, if you let it."

Lindsey Vonn

THE YEAR AFTER I moved out of the house on French Street,
while I was still in the thick of figuring out who I was and what
I was doing with my life, the mountains really took hold. I had
become a card-carrying member of Peter Pan's band of merry
misfits, an association likely to collect dues from me for a lifetime,
as it does when choosing the mountain way of life.

My job was still uninspiring, the bank account was laughable,
and my car sounded like a lawnmower, but the air was crisp, the
powder was endless, and the longer I pushed through challenges,
the more I knew the Rocky Mountains would forever be my home.

Ski days and summit hikes that had been distractions during
the early days of my season of change became more grounding.
Using my own two feet to backpack to some of the most stunning,

awe-inspiring sights I've ever seen was no longer an escape, but an integral part of a life I was starting to love.

Evenings were simple: beers on a patio, gear drying in the mudroom, conversations with new friends that felt like they'd been around forever. Somewhere among a new routine that looked a little like a vacation, I stopped questioning whether I belonged and started believing I did.

And then came Jim.

The timing of certain people showing up in our world is so interesting to me. I fully believe we maintain lifelong connections with some people, and others are meant to come and go for a specific purpose. For me, the relationship that had ended just nine months before was one of those *preparings*.

Jim and I crossed paths thanks to the community of a like-minded outdoor sport, and while that activity would later trigger our near-undoing (oh, it's coming…#chapterfour), I'm grateful it brought us together. He was, and still is, a quirky ball of adventure whose lens on life is the complete opposite of mine. He was nothing like where I had come from and in total alignment with where I seemed to be going.

Jim wasn't just a new relationship. He was an invitation.

Growing up in a teacher's house in the farmland of south-western Pennsylvania was safe and conservative in many ways. It wasn't exactly the kind of place that rears mountain climbers who venture off and live 1,600 miles away from home. And even though I had taken that leap, I was still carrying certain beliefs from my upbringing with me.

Our first photo together. The Saints won the Super Bowl that night, too. (Random.)

The "do one career for thirty years" mentality the previous generation handed down was one of those beliefs; however, in my particular childhood, there were extenuating circumstances that exacerbated both the generational norms and the culture of the geography where I was raised.

When I was five, my mom was diagnosed with a rare auto-immune disease that forced not only financial, emotional, and physical limitations on us but also formed a family dynamic that made the early days of my world small and sheltered.

Other than one trip to Rehoboth Beach the summer before Mom got sick, family vacations became short trips to the Allegheny Mountains[6] with my grandparents, aunt, and

6 "Mountains" is a generous term.

cousins. Back-to-school shopping was done in the form of layaway at Sears, and Pizza Hut was considered a fancy dinner out. Don't get me wrong, we weren't starving, and I didn't want for much. But I also didn't ask, and I knew I'd have to wait even when I did. Instant gratification was certainly not typical at the time, nor in my childhood.

As for the culture of the geography, most of my high school friends still live within twenty miles of where we grew up, and married partners from our graduating class or the year ahead of us. Claysville, Pennsylvania, is a silo that's easy to get stuck in, and that was a standard I'm pretty sure I planned to challenge the second I entered this world.

And now someone was challenging me further.

Jim pushed me to try things and let go of some of the control I had clung to for so long, even down to the fact that we were never going to be on time for anything ever again. He nudged me to say "yes" to things I would have never dreamed of doing (um, getting on a stand-up paddleboard in a Class III rapid?), to take risks I would have talked myself out of, and to let go of the rigidity I'd carried through most of life up to this point.

He made me...fun.

Fun is one of my six core values in life and business, and I can honestly say I'm not sure it would have made the list before February 6, 2010.

Infusing his love of activity and squirrel-chasing approach to life with my more boundaried, work-driven perspective brought out an adventurous spirit that had been buried under years of conditioning. For someone naturally wired to work ninety hours

December 1, 2024

Sunday Scaries Meet Your Match: Gratitude

It wouldn't be "Angie's list of gratitude" if it didn't start out with the one who turns my life into a daring adventure – Tim Callen. You can thank him for making sure I'm fed and watered and for ensuring your LinkedIn feed (and newsletters) are much less boring.

Your life partner can power (or derail) your career more than you realize, so choose wisely. The one standing next to you may just be the key to your success.

Lesson: Who supports you from behind the scenes?

a week, he sparked a sense of spontaneity to make sure I play (and I make sure he works, lol).

With him, I learned that stability doesn't mean sameness, and that love doesn't mean losing yourself, and as such, both the mountains and Jim become a necessary part of my story.

It took some time to trust he wouldn't pack up the DVDs and hit the road, and to understand that a discussion wasn't necessarily a disagreement. I still remember a pivotal conversation we had about a year and a half after we had started dating, when I was sure where things were headed and that we were on the same page.

We had backpacked to Savage Lakes, a now sadly over-discovered little gem that we had completely to ourselves. We caught fish and cooked them over the fire, watched Raia, our first dog, chase marmots, and landed on a topic you'd have thought we would have already covered.

Kids. Having children was never part of my life plan. It's not that I hate kids or hardcore never wanted them; it's because I never felt like it was something I needed to do, and no amount of societal pressure was going to change that. I thought I had clearly communicated this to Jim.

Oops.

Jim comes from a big family. No. I mean BIG family. He has thirty-nine first cousins between the two sides, and he's the oldest among all of them. Because of that, he apparently thought having kids was "something he would always do." News to me, Jim. News to me.

That fateful trip to Savage Lakes
(and your first glimpse of Raia)

Tears. So many tears. History flashed before my eyes as this non-negotiable started triggering flashbacks of packed-up apartments and more starting over. I crawled into the tent that night, sobbing without an ounce of closure, assuming the next morning we'd roll up the sleeping bags, hike out, drive home, and go our separate ways.

To my surprise, the first of exactly three romantic gestures Jim would make over our years together occurred the next morning.

"If not having kids means that I have you, then I'm ok with it."

More tears. This time, happy ones.

(In case inquiring minds need to know, Jim's other two moments of romanticism were proposing at the spot on Buttermilk where we first met and surprising me with a machete as his contribution to the cake-cutting at our wedding.)

We were on the same page and agreeing to live life on our terms — adventure, balls of fur, trials, tribulations, and all. And, man, have we made the most of it.

From the REI annex of outdoor gear in the basement to camping in countless places that required more grit than glamping. Chasing desert sunrises and summits at 4 a.m. Celebrating simple things like grounds-filled camp coffee and raising five perfect fur children, three of whom rest in peace under the fruit trees we planted in our backyard.

Pure love.

These are just some of the highlights of a life well-lived.

The girl who once measured success by stellar academics, quick promotions, and steady paychecks was finding satisfaction, fulfillment, and confidence in perfect lake reflections and laughter shared on a ridgeline, alongside a soon-to-be husband who didn't quite finish college and made a living selling wine.

What would that corporate-ladder-climbing city girl think!? I didn't care; I'm not sure I ever really did. Sure, I could have easily stayed in Boston and remained an engineer. That naive Angie would have been none the wiser — and likely be a vice president in a firm (making *bank*).

I would be fine. Four-letter F-word, F.I.N.E. fine.

Thank God I am not just fine.

You know, I've thought a lot about that word over the years.

It's the default answer to "How are you today?" And it's the thing your wife says when she's pissed and doesn't want to talk about it, but most of all, fine is a holding pattern. It's polite, safe, predictable, expected even, but it's also where dreams go to die.

The longer I stayed in the mountains, the less "fine" felt acceptable, and the less feasible it felt to go back to the city, the work, and the girl I was before. I had gotten a taste, and I wanted *more*.

More looked like waking up to pink alpenglow over snow-capped peaks and knowing my first meeting could wait until after first chair.[7] It was campfire dinners and dirt under my fingernails.

7 "First chair" translates to "early bird gets the worm" — the lift-line holy grail reserved for the crazies who get up at the ass-crack of dawn, especially coveted on a powder day.

It was trading to-do lists for trail miles, swapping screen time for desert sand. It was realizing the world wouldn't collapse if I stopped measuring my worth in the fifteen-minute increments I used to bill to projects.

More was knowing that life had a whole new way of keeping score.

What I didn't realize until much later was that finding the right place is just as important to our self-discovery as defining the right path. Rooting myself in the Rockies gave me more than a home base. It connected me to an essential sense of space that has given me room to hear myself think, become who I was meant to be, and realize the purpose I have to give to the world.

This was such an exciting time in life, not just because I had met my person, but because my expectations for life were shifting — aligning. Jim entering the picture accelerated "maybe some day" to "why not now," and "I could never" into "let's see what happens."

For the first time, I wasn't chasing the next professional milestone. I was appreciating the moment. It felt foreign, almost illegal, to slow down long enough to notice what was good and to enjoy it. What a wonderful whirlwind in so many ways. One that helped me learn how to give myself permission. To recognize the good in my life and be grateful for what I have instead of longing for the next big thing.

It took someone else — a catalyst — to give me permission first.

Eventually, I learned how to do it for myself.

Permission to play when I'd been taught to hustle.
Permission to rest when I thought I had to push.
Permission to love without worrying whether it looked respectable on a holiday card. *(For the record: flannels and jeans of questionable cleanliness are entirely acceptable for a holiday card. So is ski gear.)*
Permission to explore, take risks, do something new, unexpected, exciting.

Gratitude and permission aren't things we suddenly decide to start doing like a new workout plan.

They take repetition. And consistency, just like building any muscle. Sure, we can *say* we're thankful or *promise* to let ourselves do *the thing*, but it's just lip service until we start living it — and keep doing so. And even then, we don't find gratitude in grand gestures or permission in sweeping decisions.

We find them in small, easily overlooked moments:
The friend who shows up when we don't ask.
The Tuesday morning coffee ritual we wouldn't trade for a bigger paycheck.
The quiet **knowing** that we're on the right track, even if no one else understands it.

There's a sense of self-actualization that begins to unfold, and it gradually builds into something bigger. A way of being. Acceptance. Contentment. **Grace**.

The origin of the word grace comes from the Latin root gratis, which literally means *pleasing* and *thankful*. Isn't it amazing how gratitude and permission are so intertwined in the foundation of grace?

Yes, I just put *amazing* and *grace* in the same sentence. Coincidence? I think not.

We are so hard on ourselves today; it's no wonder we struggle to recognize what's good, let alone give ourselves the permission to choose more of it. But when we do, things start to shift, and that's because the Sunday Scaries can't compete with a grateful and gracious heart.

Just like we're not going from skiing greens to double blacks overnight, we can't expect gratitude and permission to flip a switch or act as a magic wand. They won't keep hard things from happening (duh), but they *will* remind us that we have more say in our lives than we leverage, and **that agency** is more powerful than we think.

We can't control the economy, our boss's mood, or whether our next big idea takes off on the first try, but we *can* control the perspective we bring to challenges. We control how we respond and what we do in the face of adversity.

The only way to build the kind of resilience that lets gratitude and permission stick?

Do hard things.

August 3, 2025

Add a Little Spice to Your Sunday Scaries

Every day this week, I've found myself snacking on tomatoes off the vines in our backyard garden. Who can resist a perfectly sun-ripened and satisfying pop right outside the back door!? It's funny how something so small can pack so much joy.

We forget that sometimes. In the age of the self-help craze and the urge to constantly climb a ladder, we lose sight of the significance of the little things around us.

Lesson: The tiniest things can feed you in the biggest ways.

Say the dreams out loud.

Make choices that scare us.

Walk into rooms that feel too big for us.

Hurl ourselves down a mountain bike trail for the first time at age 42.8.

Whatever your *thing* is, the one you've quietly kept from yourself, you owe it to yourself to try it.

We get one life. We can stay small, or we can choose to be grateful for the chance to live and use every bit of it to feel fulfilled and leave our mark.

I know which I choose…and I thought I understood what that choice meant.

Saying yes is the easy part. It's everything that comes after the yes that challenges our willpower. Can we stay the course? Can we continue to believe in what we've discovered about ourselves? What the manual forgets to tell us about *life on our terms* is that it doesn't mean we're bulletproof. Choices might be intentional, joyful, even courageous, but life will still throw a curveball that smacks us square in the teeth now and then.

I guess that's the point. We're not being punished. We're being prepared. Even more. And in my case, all that gratitude, permission, and grace…all that preparing…was about to get its first real test.

No More Mondays Companion Episodes

Happiness by Choice: A Google Leader's Perspective on Life Beyond Hard Work with Eric Nehrlich *(November 8, 2023)*

Balancing Mission, Mindfulness, and Margins with Jennifer Tescher *(March 15, 2023)*

Finding Meaning In The Matrix with Ricardhy Grandoit *(September 15, 2021)*

Chapter 4

BANKRUPTCY & BEN & JERRY'S

A Real Recipe for Resilience

"You never know how strong you are until
being strong is your only choice."

Bob Marley

THE FIRST REAL test came fast.

One minute, I was leaning into this new mountain life, saying yes to the relationship, the powder days, the campfire dinners, and the version of me that was starting to feel more authentic, and the next, I was staring down the kind of financial and emotional freefall they don't prepare you for in engineering school.

By June of 2010, I'd made the move, literally and figuratively, from Breckenridge to Aspen, where Jim had called home for the preceding five years. While the idea was already in my head, love was the final push to leave the CAD workstation behind for good.

I wish I could tell you I had a plan. We all know I did not. I leapt off the career-change cliff without a parachute, and somewhere midair, the first seed for my future work as a career coach was planted.

I had made it to the final round for a position with Pitkin County Open Space, which seemed like the perfect bridge out of engineering and into Aspen. Unfortunately, I found out I didn't get the job about five minutes after Jim and I hit the road for our first trip to Moab. There were a lot of tears (I've cried a lot in the last twenty pages, eh?) on that three-hour drive, but Moab has always had a way of grounding me, and over time, it would become a place we return to often to reset.

Upon our return, I had a newfound sense of resolve to make the move work. We can go ahead and call the spade the spade here. What I would love to deem determination was really desperation, and that rarely works out well for a job seeker.

I took the first job that came along: running a single artist's gallery in downtown Aspen. I traded blueprints for brush-strokes, stability for uncertainty, and a steady engineering salary for…well, not that.

Breaking the news to my parents that I wasn't going to remain in engineering was its own special kind of hell. My mom didn't speak to me for three weeks, the longest silence between us since the night I arrived on December 10, 1980, two weeks early and already, clearly, stubborn. (For the record, she's my biggest

fan; she just needed a minute to catch up to my life choices —
didn't we all?)

This whole gallery thing treated me pretty well for a while.
I got to hobnob with the elite (looking behind the curtain of the
1 percent can definitely give you a complex!). I hosted gallery
openings, toasted millionaires with champagne, and saw a stack
of fresh out-of-a-safe hundies wrapped in paper stamped $10,000
for the first time. It's all about the Benjamins, baby.

Let's make a toast to the gallery openings!

I skied seventy days that season, and wined and dined at
some of Aspen's finest hot spots thanks to Jim's wine perks and
work expense account. The Great Recession took its time sinking
into the insulated and elite bubble that is Aspen.

But, eventually…it hit.

Turns out selling expensive paintings in a recession is about as stable as building sandcastles in the tide. The "lucrative opportunity" the outgoing gallery director promised never materialized, and before long, I was dipping into the *would-have-been-a-millionaire-by-now* 401(k) we don't talk about in our house.

Jim, a certified sommelier,[8] was still working in wine shops, restaurants, and distributing bottles, none of which were any more reliable as the recession's effects became increasingly evident in our tourist-driven economy.

And then, just like that, ten months into the art walks, openings, and champagne toasts, the gallery closed. Overnight, it was gone. My first experience of losing a job I hadn't chosen to leave had me questioning every ounce of value I had to provide the world. I won't lie, there's a certain amount of pride that's swallowed when, as a former engineer with a degree from Carnegie Mellon, you find yourself on the unemployment line.

Enter rock bottom numero dos. I was staring down the identity crisis I'd "successfully avoided" for the past year, and the only way I knew how to cope was to sit on the couch with my fifth pint of Ben & Jerry's of the week.

Change is a funny thing. We say we want it, but most never chase it. Others are averse to it. And then there are people like me who embrace change only to discover that the destination isn't always what we pictured… and that the road between is full of potholes no one warns you about.

8 A sommelier (pronounced soh-muh-lyay) is a certified wine expert, a.k.a the overachiever who turned "drinking on the job" into a career.

August 24, 2025

Midweek Momentum versus The Sunday Scaries

We've all heard it, and we've all said it. "I thought I'd failed," or worse, "I feel like a failure."

Reinvention isn't failure, it's evolution, and in that moment when everything feels like it's over, we get a turning point – a catalyst often needed to see things differently and build something bigger and better than we would have been able to otherwise.

💡 Lesson: Rock bottom can be the exact push you need.

When I left Boston for Breck, friends — especially ski friends — would say things like, "I'm jealous. You're living my dream." My response was always the same: "I'm no one special. You could do this, too." Now? Unemployed. Broke. Wondering if I'd just made the biggest mistake of my life.

Who on Earth would be jealous of me now?

The fact of the matter is that I'd made choices that took both my lifestyle and my career outside of the norm. My future no longer included a corporate ladder, suburban cul-de-sac, or a respectable growth path that people could understand, and it felt like it was catching up with me. I had to wonder if I was gritty enough to see it through, to keep living this nontraditional life when it wasn't so shiny…or sustainable. Mountain adventure can fill a lot of your soul, but unless you're an elite athlete with 23 X Games medals, your outdoor pursuits aren't putting food on the table.

At this point, the Sunday Scaries were no longer reserved for one day a week. They were creeping in on Tuesday mornings when I didn't have anywhere to be, Thursday afternoons when the phone wasn't ringing, or in the grocery store line when I realized the Manager's Special beef was the smart option. The fear wasn't just about money, though the dwindling dollar signs were hard to ignore.

It was the deeper question: *What if I can't recover from this?*

I didn't have an answer to that question, and would ask myself that same thing at several points in the future (don't worry, there's plenty of rock bottom to come). But, thankfully, I was tossed a lifeline. It wasn't glamorous, but it was a buoy.

A local nonprofit needed part-time help, which was enough to cover the bills while I figured out my next move. I still laugh when I think about the day the executive director called to offer me the job. We were in Virginia Beach on vacation with Jim's (entire massive) family when the call came: "We'd like to hire you, but you are grossly overqualified for this." *No kidding, hon. No kidding.*

My experience with the nonprofit world was minimal — actually nonexistent — until that point, and suddenly I was immersed in it. The reality? A complete toxic circus. I'm not sure how a workplace of seven people can create so much drama, but, as my grandmother would say, that air was so thick, you could cut it with a butter knife. The poster child for a "this is how it's always been done" environment doesn't jive well with growth-oriented, push-boundaries Angie, but somehow I found a silver lining within the terrible culture.

A little thing called turnover.

That place had a revolving door of staff cycling in and out faster than a ski bum through off-season leases, and that spelled opportunity for me. Within a year, I worked my way from part-time admin to Director of Operations and Events, a role that set me up for a move to a different nonprofit, in what became my first senior leadership position: executive director of a high-visibility, grassroots community organization. That's where things started to shift.

The work wasn't just a job, but an awakening that stirred what I now know was an entrepreneurial spirit that had been dying to come out. I was creating programs, expanding the organization's reach, building partnerships, and, for the first time, feeling like I was making a meaningful impact.

I was also being recognized for it, with articles in luxury Aspen magazines, styled photo shoots where I got to wear $8,000 necklaces, and a spot on Aspen's list of ten most influential leaders. I was on top of the world in every sense. New identity, new purpose, and a new fire that would eventually lead me to build my own thing, but we've got a lot more life to get through first.

My personal life was going great during this time, too. Jim and I tied the knot in the fall of 2012, about six months before I took the executive director position. We got married at the one and only Frank Lloyd Wright's Fallingwater in Pennsylvania.

All the feels on October 21, 2012.

We also added a second dog, Foster, to the family, and settled into life on the little homesteading farm where we rented the apartment above the garage. My career kept climbing, Jim bounced between restaurant gigs (as one does in that world of volatility), and we made it work.

We had found our footing. But, in true "us" fashion, a big choice was waiting around the corner, ready to flip everything upside down.

Anyone else sensing a theme?

In 2015, we bought a business. On paper, it seemed like a no-brainer. It was tied to the way Jim and I first met, so there was a certain romance to it. It felt like the perfect opportunity to blend our skills while providing Jim a more stable-than-food-and-beverage career track.

My leadership and operations background. His outdoor industry expertise. A seasonal business he could run while I still held my position at the nonprofit. We told ourselves it was a "natural next step" toward building something of our own.

Now, I'll pause and tell you that hindsight is a pretty incredible thing. So is your gut. If you want the TL;DR (too long; didn't read for anyone over the age of thirty-nine), I'll just tell you this thing was doomed from the minute we ever mentioned the idea to each other, but that doesn't make for a very tantalizing read.

Too stubborn to see the signs and take multiple funding nos for an answer, we eventually found a way to finance the purchase. An SBA loan served as the down payment to the previous owner and founder, who then carried a promissory note for the remaining balance (seller-financed). I still remember the day we drove over to Breckenridge to sign the papers and make it official.

That day in May 2015 will live in infamy as the day we made a single decision that (could have) ruined our entire lives. Hell, it came close to doing just that. I'll leave you hanging on the edge of your seat with that teaser, but I will let you in on how the day transpired.

Remember that **_knowing_** I mentioned a while back when I was settling into Colorado life? Well, it came back full force the day that we signed the papers to acquire this business.

My gut, my bones, and even my brain told me that day that we shouldn't proceed. I had an inkling. A feeling. A sixth sense that it was a bad idea. There was a feeling of foreboding on the entire drive over to the attorney's office, but I kept it to myself. Did nothing. Said nothing.

The feeling that we were too far into things to back out took over, so we did what we were "supposed" to do.

Transaction complete. We signed the papers, moved a garage full of inventory two hours west along I-70, and made a cute little video introducing us as the new owners of this beloved community-centric business.

At first, it was exciting. Imagining freedom, strategizing for growth, reveling in the pride of calling something ours, but none

September 14, 2024

Get Surgical with Your Sunday Scaries

Healing isn't linear, neither is life. We can do everything "right" and still face setbacks we never saw coming.

The truth is, resilience isn't a straight climb back to normal. It's a winding trail, full of switchbacks, steep sections, and unexpected detours. Sometimes it even feels like we're walking in circles..

💡 Lesson: Growth is rarely a straight line, so focus on one step at a time.

of it was enough to cover the cracks we didn't see before we signed on the dotted line.

In less than two years, the business nearly destroyed us, financially, emotionally, relationally, and in ways that will never fully be captured in the pages of this book. What I can tell you is that by the end, we were standing in a bankruptcy attorney's office, defending a last-resort decision that felt like the most public declaration of failure I'd ever experienced.

If only that were the case, but I digress...

We had been sold a bill of goods.

A steaming pile of shit.

Don't get me wrong, I know we saw what we wanted to see. But I attribute the outcome just as much to our naivety as to shifty reporting that hid a sudden and drastic change in financial performance.

We paid for that mistake. Dearly.

We've all heard the term
what doesn't kill us makes us stronger.

I can tell you with absolute certainty that it is an accurate statement. A hard truth, but a truth nonetheless, and out of it comes resilience, the courage to continue, the faith to trust again.

When I interview other entrepreneurs on the *No More Mondays* podcast, our conversations almost always circle back to rock-bottom stories. We all have them, and while many of us make it our mission to help others avoid that kind of fallout, the reality is that those experiences shape us in ways nothing else can.

They build perspective.
They thicken our skin.
They reveal our purpose.

Yes, some choices will break us. Not because we're weak or reckless, but because the outcome was never ours to control in the first place. We can do the homework, run the numbers, and still get blindsided by the variables we couldn't see, were hidden from view, or were otherwise ignored.

Courage isn't about making the perfect choice. It's about making *a* choice, knowing it could hurt like hell, and still showing up even if it does. It's getting out of bed in the middle of a collapse and doing what we can with what's left, even when "what's left" doesn't look like much.

That's where resilience kicks in.

Resilience isn't about bouncing back to the way it was before. That's just never-gonna-happen. That phase of our lives is gone, and so is the version of the person who lived it.

That doesn't mean we go down with the ship. Real resilience is absorbing the hit, grieving what's gone, and then starting again with whatever pieces we can salvage, even if they feel flawed and incomplete. It's not about recreating the past but about building something new that can hold the weight of who we've become.

My little friends, grit and grace, are in there, too, working quietly to keep us moving while resilience takes root, helping through the day-in, day-out choice to take one more step forward, then another, and another until momentum builds and a new direction begins to emerge.

These are the emotions, maybe even the tools, that we need to make it through hard times. They don't just help us survive; they give us the chance to create something better than what we lost. To mount our comeback. To be the best version of ourselves.

If you've ever found yourself in your own version of a bankruptcy attorney's office, that rock-bottom moment that feels like it will define you for the rest of your life, remember this: **we are more than our darkest moments.** The worst decision we've ever made doesn't blacklist us from a fulfilling future. A human cannot be a failure. Mistakes do not define us.

What we do after the bottom falls out is where the real story begins, and if there's one thing I've learned through my journey to thicker skin, it's that we're more resilient — and more capable — than we think.

No More Mondays Companion Episodes

Entrepreneurship Beyond the Money: Defining Success on Your Own Terms with Justin Schenck *(February 17, 2025)*

Where Do I Go from Here? Reinventing Yourself after Your Whole World Crumbles with Jennifer Arthurton *(May 16, 2023)*

Chapter 5

UNHOUSED, UNTITLED, UNAPOLOGETIC

The Road Back to Authenticity

"You are so brave and quiet, I forget you are suffering."

Ernest Hemingway

IF YOU THOUGHT bankruptcy was the bottom, let me assure you, it was not.

As a couple who chose to have pets instead of human children, our tragedies multiplied. Within the year that followed, we lost our cat. Jax, and yes, part of Jim's "dowry," and put our first dog, Raia, through five major surgeries in an attempt to save her from an aggressive cancer that seemed to grow back overnight.

There wasn't a single bastion of hope on any area of the home front, and that included our actual home. I'm not talking about the emotional, relational kind, although walking on eggshells is inevitable when you and your husband have just gone through complete financial ruin.

Post-surgery snuggles

I mean the literal, roof-over-your-head type of home.

The homesteading farm we'd treated as our own for nearly a decade, where we cared for goats, chickens, rabbits, ducks, and vegetables like they were our own, got yanked out from under us with less than thirty days' notice.

If I thought being unemployed and broke was bad, now I was homeless and bankrupt, with two giant dogs in a rental market that barely had vacancies for someone with an 850 credit score, let alone this hot mess. We had little to no income coming in because I had stepped away from the nonprofit I'd been leading in the midst of the bankruptcy shitstorm, so we were living on tips from Jim's shifts slinging drinks at the bar a few times a week.

Whoever said things come in threes was full of it; this was feeling like the onset of world's sixth mass extinction event.

Somewhere in the middle of this mess, I did the most logical thing someone can do in the midst of a total life disaster: I started a business.

One month after bankruptcy, somewhere between pints of *Everything But The...*(and the pants that were getting a little snug) and a few months before we lost the roof over our heads, I had scribbled the first notes for a little idea.

A company called Career Benders.

It would turn out to be the desperation-triggered decision that turned everything around, but first, we needed a home.

During our short-lived days of business ownership, we had a Ford van that carried us (and way too much inventory) up and down I-70.[9] When things started to go south, I began looking for every possible economic way to keep us in the mountains

The pandemic-era vanlife craze had yet to hit the social influencer circuit, but somehow I stumbled into the Pinterest rabbit hole of tiny living. Jim was staunchly opposed to the idea that the solution to all our pre-bankruptcy financial woes would be found by cramming two humans and two sixty-plus-pound dogs into a van.

I kept pinning anyway. The obsession escalated from Sprinter vans to converted school buses, which had just started to emerge in the micro-tiny-house world. And there, my middle-aged

9 I-70: sanity sold separately.

woman's love of Pinterest collided with our desperate need for a roof over our heads.

Skoolies.

I still remember where we were when I looked at Jim, the clock ticking on our housing situation and options running out fast, and said, half-joking, "Maybe we should just do the bus thing."

To my surprise, he didn't laugh. "Maybe we should."

The van that triggered the Great Skoolie Spiral.

We gave ourselves two weeks to explore the idea. Those two weeks were spent obsessively refreshing Craigslist, Facebook Marketplace, and bus-dedicated forums, scheming about how we'd tow a school bus across the country on a shoestring budget, while half-seriously considering whether Jim's parents would notice if we parked a forty-footer in their driveway for a month.

Spoiler: the "find a cheap bus in New Jersey and figure it out later" plan didn't make it past day two.

But lucky day number thirteen delivered, and twenty-four hours before the plan would have shifted from getting a bus across the country to moving *us* across the country, a listing popped up.

In Colorado Springs.

For exactly the amount of money in our bank account.

And you don't believe someone up there is watching out for you...?

Within twenty-four hours, we were the proud owners of a 1989 Bluebird International sixty-six-passenger bus, the same kind we Xennials rode in first grade. By some miracle, it had already been gutted and was just waiting to be made into a home.

We just did what?

Rio, as she would be called, made her maiden voyage over Independence Pass[10] with Jim at the wheel, two dogs (one mid-cancer treatment) rolling around in the cavernous steel shell, complete with sheets of metal rattling around. Oh, and the side mirrors were on upside down and backward. The rest of that story entails a vehicle length restriction, a cop, and a horse trailer, but that's best told 'round a campfire with some whiskey.

She rolled into the Roaring Fork Valley on October 4, 2018, and we had twenty-six days to make her "livable" before vacating our apartment and winter in the Rockies set in.

Turning a thirty-year-old school bus into a full-time tiny home is the DIY project of a lifetime, and for those three-and-a-half weeks, Jim worked on the bus like it was his only job. Well, because it was. I was slinging career coaching services as if my life depended on it — because it did — and in between clients, I was cutting plywood, rolling paint, or pulling midnight insulation shifts.

Every time I closed a client, I'd yell, "Nine hundred bucks! What's next?" and off to Lowe's we would go. Insulation? Composting toilet? Electrical? The DeWalt driver Jim swore was essential? The bus ate money like a teenager eats pizza — fast and without apology — and I funneled every dollar I could into keeping the project and our dreams of staying in Colorado alive.

---

10 A stunning high-elevation mountain pass that tops out at 12,095 feet, famous for breathtaking views, harrowing switchbacks, and an eerily narrow width that makes even a Prius driver hold their breath.

When I say every dime went into the bus build, I mean that our meals consisted of eating root vegetables out of a five-gallon bucket we had filled during the last harvest from the garden. Parsnips, carrots, and a scant potato, plus you guessed it, some Manager's Special beef, and we were set for a night or two.

Come to think of it, the dogs were eating better than we were.

I'm happy to report it was worth it. Mission accomplished. Halloween night, thirty-two degrees, snowing...we moved into our construction site on wheels.

No heat.
No running water.
No toilet.
Lots of charm.

Our Christmas gift to each other that year was a Tiny Wood Stove (yes, that's the brand name, and yes, they're worth a follow on Instagram). It became our main heat source, and a four-year bat signal that Angie and Jim had arrived, with signature scent: Eau de Campfire, in tow.

It took us three months to get to the point where I could install basic plumbing, and another month after that before the water was hot. The kettle we used for coffee got a lot of miles during those few months. But we gradually unlocked new levels: the luxury of seven-minute military showers, a glorified toaster oven, an actual refrigerator, and something that looked less like a mobile storage unit and more like a micro home.

And yes, I became a pro at making a hair wash last a week (a skill I may or may not have maintained…)

Before Pink Floyd was a Sunday River hoodie bought around 2004. It didn't survive the bus build… but luckily, these two did.

Our family changed quickly after making the bus home, which Raia got to enjoy for only a few short weeks. She crossed the Rainbow Bridge on December 11, 2018, one day after our shared birthday. She was special, the loss was potent, and sadly, due to all life was handing us at the time, I'm not sure I was emotionally present enough to fully feel it.

I kept moving because stopping meant feeling — *everything* — and that was a luxury I couldn't afford at the time. Only later did I come to realize how much we'd lost…and also how much we had somehow survived.

The dog, the job, the house, the dignity. The fact that we were living a Billboard Top 100 country song had become more humorous than humiliating, even if we hadn't hit full recovery mode yet.

There were still plenty of fires to put out, but at least the feeling of constant freefall had waned. The grief of losing Raia was real, but there was also a strange sense of peace in realizing we had weathered the storm (tsunami?) and landed, of all places, in this ridiculous 1989 school bus.

I swear, we'll be eighty years old and will still be "the bus people" at every wedding we attend.

Living in a bus, it turns out, makes you the talk of the table in just about every social situation. It also forces you to minimize, and it's amazing how much you don't actually need when you don't have space to store it. Every item had to earn its keep. Every decision was about survival and simplicity: fill the clean water, empty the greywater, grab two days' worth of groceries, and chop enough wood to keep the fingers warm enough for typing.

I couldn't make this stuff up if I tried, and even then, I'd struggle to write a more absurd set of lyrics to that aforementioned country song. Backwards or forwards, I wasn't getting the dog, a full-height house, or my bougie career in Aspen back any time soon. Makes it perfectly logical that I was selling boutique, high-ticket career coaching…from a bus, eh?

January 5, 2025

150 Weeks of Leaving the Sunday Scaries Behind

Over the years, we've shared tips that cover everything from cleaning out a junk drawer to streamlining packed schedules and reevaluating relationships.

The bottom line? Create space for what really matters. Simplifying isn't just about getting rid of things; it's about giving yourself room to breathe, focus, and alleviate the disruptions that keep us from thriving.

💡 Lesson: Set a timer for fifteen minutes and declutter one area each day this week.

"Hello, let me help you negotiate that six-figure salary as soon as I take down the laundry strung across the room of my seeming Depression-era homestead."

I'd gone from board meetings and glossy magazine spreads to hauling five-gallon jugs of water up icy steps, balancing dinner on a single cast-iron pan, and supporting executives from the safety of a Zoom room where I blurred the Pink Panther insulation behind me while praying the smell of s'mores didn't give me away at the next Denver networking event.

The irony of coaching people into confident career moves while patching together survival in a 225-square-foot home, with no running water, questionable hygiene, and a very tired marriage, was definitely *not* lost on me.

For so long, my identity had been tethered to titles: Engineer. Director. Executive. Even the ill-fated "Business Owner" carried clout...before she didn't.

I was recognizable and recognized as a leader in any of those ecosystems. And now? I was just Angie: a woman in a bus, carrying around the ashes of her dead cat and dog, and career coaching in a Pink Floyd hoodie flecked in spray foam and paint samples.

If you've seen that hoodie, you know you're in a different class (wink).

The community I'd once led looked at me sideways. No, that's not quite fair. Full-on hostile. Former customers, once friends, associated Jim and me with the wreckage of the failed business, and to this day, I'm sure more than a few still consider us the spawns of Satan.

For someone who loves connections, craves people, and finds meaning in community, my circle had been shrunk to one: Jim.

As you can imagine, there was plenty of tension in our physically tiny circle for two. I mean, you try surviving bankruptcy, pet death, home loss, and living in the active construction zone that is your bus conversion without killing each other.

By some miracle, we're not only both alive, but we came out stronger. Jim and I worked through the trauma, resentment, and pain together, without therapy, and while living, quite literally, on top of each other. And people say buying a house together is the hardest thing a couple goes through.

All was well and good, except for one little thing. **This girl** was still trying to figure out who *that guy* actually married.

Everything I had worked for, every marker of success I thought defined me, had been stripped away. My résumé read like a cautionary tale that only the local City Market dared touch (I know because I was hired on as a grocery picker for a hot minute, until I realized their version of "part-time" was a fifty-five-hour week).

Career Benders was beginning to take shape, but at this point, it wasn't an anchor.

It was a lifeline held together by just a few strands.
A Hail Mary.
Hope.

I hadn't yet built the credibility or reputation to stand on it with confidence, so I found myself straddling two worlds: one foot planted in basic human survival, the other stretching for untapped potential that seemed just beyond reach.

I wasn't incompetent, far from it. I was helping people. I was delivering results. But I was also living the truest, most extreme version of imposter syndrome the doc has ever seen. Career coaching high-level professionals out of a gutted school bus while trying to reassemble the shambles of my once-promising career.

If irony were currency, I could have paid off my student loans around page fifteen.

Ah, the trap. As many of us know, impostor syndrome isn't really about our abilities, but knowing that and *believing* it are two very different things.

As my friend Kris Kelso says in his book, *Overcoming the Impostor: Silence Your Inner Critic and Lead with Confidence*, "Impostor Syndrome is not a reflection of your ability, it's a distortion of your perception."

Oh, was my perception distorted! My clients weren't questioning me. I was questioning myself. They saw value; I saw plywood, pink insulation, and a hoodie that smelled like ash.

Bus or no bus, I know you can relate. Admit it. That imposter syndrome has crept in somewhere. In fact, 62 percent of us will experience imposter syndrome at some point in our lives.[11] It could show up in the boardroom where we feel like we don't belong, the meeting where we hold back the big idea, or the moment we land the promotion and immediately think, *they're going to find me out.*

While the perception we have of ourselves in these moments is false, the tension between that perception and reality is real, and that's what pulled me into an Olympic-level wrestling match.

That's the thing about imposter syndrome. It doesn't care how smart, successful, or self-aware we are; in fact, studies show it hits people like us even more frequently! There's no "logicing" our way out of the feeling.

I just had to live my way through it, and somehow, bus life, in all its stripped-down, uncomfortable, humbling glory, is what miraculously gave me the *space* to tackle these questions.

Tackle the uncertainty. Tackle myself.

Lost labels. Squashed reputation. Shame. Who was I? Where was the happy-go-lucky mountain girl who hopped, skipped, and jumped out of engineering and into Aspen? Where was the party-throwing gallery director who convinced a gazillionaire they needed another painting on their mansion walls? Where was the girl on the cover of the magazine?

It didn't matter because I wasn't that girl. At least not anymore, maybe not ever. Even as the mountains were revealing my own truths, I realized I still had never landed on who I was

11 Multiple meta-analyses and reviews of more than thirty studies estimate that 60–70 percent of people experience imposter syndrome at some point (see, for example, Bravata et al., *Journal of General Internal Medicine*, 2020). Statistically speaking, we're all "faking it until we make it."

without performance and achievement, and now, in the cold, cramped, barely insulated walls of a bus, I was starting to find her.

Angie. Without the titles. Without comfort. Without the external validation.

I had been forced back to basics (and to Chapter One), left to my own devices to figure out who I was when there was no impressive, ambitious thing to prop me up. In the tiniest and most unexpected of places, big discoveries emerged.

What showed up when all of that was gone was authenticity.

The downfall, the crash, living "big" in a tiny bus — none of it was glamorous, but it forced me to stop performing for everyone else and start figuring out what it actually meant to be myself. It kinda sucks that it took losing just about everything I *thought* carried meaning to get there.

Then again, how else can we arrive at the needed conclusion that identity is about who we are when there's nothing left to prove?

Back in Chapter One, we talked about how easy it is to stay *fine,* to keep ourselves small, to accept the mediocrity that society considers normal. It's easy to do what's expected, to wear the labels we're handed: titles, achievements, job descriptions, family roles.

July 21, 2024

Stay Chill: Sunday Scaries Solutions

Mindset is critical to progress. Finding a way to maintain positivity and shut out those nasty, lying voices created by imposter syndrome is crucial to your success.

Positive affirmations, gratitude, and just plain looking at the facts are all productive ways to quiet that little devil.

💡 Lesson: Gather your receipts and prove you are more capable than the imposter says!

But those labels aren't who we are; they're what we do.

The two are not the same, and imposter syndrome feeds on the space between. Authenticity, on the other hand, is what closes the gap. It allows *who we are* to lead and *what we do* to follow, and that's when the Sunday Scaries start to lose their grip.

It doesn't matter how successful we are, how much money we have, or the number of followers we've racked up; the gap can still appear. Even the most values-aligned entrepreneurs living their dream are still *someone* beyond the brands they've built, the products they've launched, and the impact they've made.

Professional athletes, household names, your favorite influencer — they're all *someone* underneath the pads, behind the mic, and beyond highlight reels. That does not mean they're a whole different person entirely; it means they know how to show up as themselves in different contexts.

Authenticity isn't about being the same in every setting; it's about being self-aware enough to adapt without losing yourself. That's what emotional intelligence really is — knowing who you are, no matter the room you're in, and letting that awareness guide how you relate to and connect with others. Authenticity informs *how* we present ourselves, but it does not allow us to *shape-shift* to meet someone else's expectations.

The Sunday Scaries creep in when we forget that. When we start performing for approval instead of showing up with intention, that's when our sense of self begins to hinge on the outcome rather than the effort, and what we *do for work* starts to define who we *are as humans*.

If you're lucky, like I was, you get a bus to remind you that you're more than a business card, but you don't need a Tiny Wood Stove, greasy hair, or your own version of rock bottom to figure this out.

It starts by creating space.

I really do hope you smirked, or at least rolled your eyes at that impressive bit of irony. But I'm not talking about an extra five square feet (that would have felt like a dream). I'm talking about mental space; the bandwidth to separate the profession from the person. To notice when and how those wires might have gotten crossed.

Sometimes that space looks like solitude. Sometimes it looks like silence. Most of the time, it looks like simply paying attention to:

Labels. Look at the titles, roles, or achievements you introduce yourself with most often. Are you inextricably tied to them? Do they provide more value than they should? Would you still know who you are without them?

Quirks. Your identity is often tucked in the places you think are "too weird" to mention; the Pink Floyd hoodie covered in spray foam, the terrible analogies and dad jokes, the hobby you've been hiding because it's not "productive." Lean in and own what makes you, you.

"Who," not "what." The next time someone asks, "What do you do?" answer with a piece of who you are, not just "I'm an engineer." We'll take a note out of Jim's book here: "I mountain bike in the summer and ski in the winter!" Yep, people look at him quizzically, but they'll remember…and it usually leads to an interesting conversation.

The Pull. Where do you feel like you're performing? Where do you feel like you're keeping yourself small? Where do you feel like you're saying the thing you think someone wants to hear? Those are signs you're getting pulled out of alignment with your authenticity and true identity.

Lean into one of the above this week. Pick a label, a quirk, or a pull, and pay attention to it. Go into the woods where there's no service, and you have no choice but to be alone with your thoughts, and notice how it feels. How it feels to let them go. To say something different. To take on a definition outside of the thing you do.

The realizations that come out of this exercise may feel trivial, but they'll be meaningful because they're a start.

But why does it even matter?

Because if we don't take the time to proactively understand who we are, what we value, and what exists when everything else is stripped away, we will eventually face a crisis of identity.

My version of that crisis hit just about every aspect of my being, and I've seen that in others, too. Parenting, for example, can be so all-consuming that when year eighteen hits, some moms and dads suddenly realize they don't know who they are beyond their caregiver role. For you, it may be something else entirely, but the danger is the same.

Work, family, titles, they all matter, but none of them is the whole story.

Our story is the one where meaning takes center stage. Where we become energized instead of drained by the things we pour ourselves into. Where we walk into rooms grounded in who we are and what we bring, not necessarily what we've achieved or the title we hold.

That's the real power of authenticity: it's not putting on a happy face or attempting to be over-the-top original. It's about alignment. Being genuine. It's being unapologetically you, not for shock value or performance (because sorry that isn't authentic), but because it's simply the *only* way you know how to *be*.

And that brings me to the million-dollar question to wrap up this chapter:

Who are you when you stop trying to be everything to everyone (else)?

That's where the Sunday Scaries stop, and a meaningful life begins. When you can answer that question, the labels will fade away, and the pressure to perform will lose its appeal. Alignment falls into place.

It's when you stop managing your life and start *living* it.

Most importantly, it's when the
real you finally gets a say.

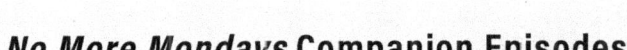

No More Mondays Companion Episodes

Discovering Authenticity: How Adam McChesney Found Success Through Personal Branding *(February 3, 2025)*

Go Minimalist to Maximize: How to Come Back from Burnout with Shannon Arner *(March 1, 2023)*

Chapter 6

CLOSETS, COFFEE, AND CORE VALUES

By Default or By Design

"Those who have a 'why' to live, can
bear with almost any 'how.'"

Viktor Frankl

FOR A STRETCH of years, Denver became my second home.
Two, sometimes three times a month, I'd leave the valley at
5 a.m. and make the three-and-a-half-hour drive east, chasing
every opportunity I could to get Career Benders off the ground.

I'd roll straight into a string of whatever was semi-humanly
possible to cram into forty-eight hours: coffee meetups, client
sessions, and back-to-back networking events, where I quickly
learned you don't drive from Thornton to Lone Tree at 4 p.m.
unless you want to spend the night on I-25.[12]

---

12 For the non-Coloradans: a worse fate would only be found if you were stuck in
China's twelve-day, sixty-two-mile traffic jam in 2010.

I shook hands, traded cards, ate more gluten-free pancakes than IHOP thought anyone could want, and pitched myself in every way I knew how. By the time the day was over, I'd collapse wherever I could.

Sometimes that meant pulling into a hotel parking lot at 11 p.m. and unrolling my Therm-a-Rest® in the back of my Subaru. Other times, it was a $39 room in a shared Airbnb, which ranged from pot-filled basements with impromptu jam sessions to reclusive hosts who seemed allergic to eye contact. I bet they were engineers…

Eventually, I upgraded from the trunk of the car to an office, and by office, I mean a glorified closet above a total Millennial-hipster boutique full of Z Supply and Kenzie jeans.

Closet or office? You decide.

A desk, a coffee pot, and an air mattress crammed into a bench pretty much felt like the big time after a little too much time sleeping in vehicles. I mean, even if one is remodeled into a home, it still has four wheels.

My secret outpost. By day, a neutral place to meet clients. By night, my little home away from my tiny home.

The lack of posh was admirable, and yet again, made for one hell of a paradox. Thus continues my clear theme of irony. Coaching executives on career strategy in the afternoon, then brushing my teeth in a parking lot before crawling into the trunk of a fifteen-year-old Outback with 200,000 miles on it.

Good thing it was a hatchback. And I'm only five-one.

If imposter syndrome had been dogging me in the bus, this was my way of laughing in its face. What's more ridiculous? Living in a gutted school bus or sleeping in your car between networking breakfasts?

I'll leave you to decide.

The truth is, the grind wasn't about where to sleep; it was what I packed into those trips. I was in full-on hustle mode, and there was nothing I wasn't willing to do to make Career Benders work.

Hello, bootstrapping!

A term typically used in the tech world, where a lot more money is concerned, it definitely applied here. Most people would hire help, buy ads, or invest in shortcuts. That would have been nice, but those options involved money. I didn't have that, so I invested what I did have: time, energy, and a personality, even if the effort drained every ounce of me.

By the time I finally made it home, a trip that seemingly involved a snowstorm regardless of whether it was January or June, I would crash for three days straight. Exhausted doesn't even cover it, even for an extreme extrovert who loves to work a room.

But all that effort was earning me something I hadn't had in years: momentum, and with it, a missing piece I hadn't realized I'd been craving: belonging.

I made friends in those circles who are still part of my corner today, people who heard the story, ugly parts and all, and accepted me anyway. After years of shame, crumbling communities, and being outcast, my sense of belonging was being renewed.

That belonging built confidence — and traction.

Career Benders wasn't just an idea anymore. It was starting to take root.

Every drive, every handshake, every sleepless night in the Outback or glorified closet moved me further from proof of concept and closer to progress. Clients were showing up. Word was spreading, and for the first time since everything fell apart, the numbers began to move in the right direction.

By the end of 2018, while we were still hammering away at bus walls and praising the addition of "heat," Career Benders managed to muster a total revenue of about $40,000. We'll call it the "proof of concept" year, which was enough to make me think, *Okay, maybe I can actually make a living at this.*

The following year, we not only filled in any last visible traces of the Pink Panther insulation on the walls, but we also found a fantastic home base for the bus, and I managed to double the revenue of the previous year. Proof of concept, not so much. *I'm onto something.*

In January of 2020, I remember telling Jim that it was time to scale back on the Denver trips. Not only were they exhausting, but the windshield time was seriously eating into available client meetings I couldn't afford to lose. By then, I had a networking base, referrals, and a reputation strong enough that I no longer needed the "first coffee meeting in person" hook.

A month later, the universe helped me out…

I know that many businesses have a "pandemic pivot" story, and perhaps this sounds like one of them. But for me, it wasn't about pivoting; it was about being perfectly positioned. People were questioning their careers, and I had already built the foundation to help find some answers.

And the floodgates opened.

Jim was on an extended river trip on the Upper Salt River in Arizona in March of 2020 and returned to a world that had changed overnight. Meanwhile, I was sitting with this "little" business of mine that had gone from hope-and-a-prayer to steaming locomotive, picking up speed by the day.

I had considered bringing on help, but a global pandemic is a big fat pause button to any small-business owner making big decisions, so I kept chugging along…and chug I did. Any amount of uncertainty I had didn't last long, as the global crisis triggered a newfound sense of purpose in people. If they didn't like where they were in life, they sure as hell wanted to get somewhere better before the world ended.

Thus, career coaching crashed onto the scene, and I was primed to ride the wave.

By December, my lifeline of a business had exploded to $250,000 in revenue in just two years. My Hail Mary, my hope, had become a powerhouse.

And I was the single fuel keeping the machine running.

For about six months, I coached forty hours a week. No, I didn't *work* forty hours a week; I **coached** forty hours a week, a pace no one should attempt, not even a high-energy people-lover. I was burning the candle at both ends, six-day workweeks, twelve hours a day, and the wick was getting thin.

Résumé bullets were scribbled in five minutes between clients, pee breaks doubled as "Sorry, I'm two minutes late to Zoom." If I were lucky, I'd remember to eat something while hunkered down in the windowless coworking office I'd rented near the bus (what's up with that no natural light trend?).

Labor Day hit, and I miraculously managed to take a long weekend, so Jim and I escaped on a twenty-mile multi-day backpacking trip to Capitol and Moon Lakes. Fall of 2020. I've never seen that many people in the backcountry. Sheesh. We even watched a helicopter rescue from Capitol Peak[13] overnight. Spooky.

13 Capitol Peak: one of Colorado's notorious 14ers, famous for its "Knife's Edge" — a 150-foot-long, one-foot-wide granite ridge where "don't look down" becomes less of a suggestion and more of a survival strategy. Translation: a peak Angie will never climb. You're welcome, Mom.

*Somewhere around mile fourteen of twenty
of that Labor Day backpacking trip (escape).*

*Tim and Foster are making use of the
dowry several years later, lol.*

The trip was simultaneously rejuvenating, exhausting, and revealing. I came back more aware than ever that I was pouring everything I had into everyone else while never stopping to refill my cup.

I was running on fumes, and this powerhouse I was building was going to implode if I kept up this pace. It was time to stop letting this business control me and turn the tables around. I had pushed as hard as I could, and the truth was undeniable: something had to give.

The following year was all about unraveling. Not in a bad way, but in the way you have to when you've spun yourself up so tightly that you barely have a minute to think. We integrated Jim into the business (yay, no more restaurants), implemented *Profit First*, and hired an executive assistant. I gave more hours to my part-time marketer, raised my prices, and started drawing real boundaries around my time.

Back to business basics…and it worked. My work quality improved (almost as much as my quality of life!), client relationships strengthened, referrals increased, and the business became stronger and more sustainable. I guess there's truth to that whole thing about building a solid foundation before you try to throw a house on top.

The momentum I'd built was impressive — borderline feral, really — exhilarating and unsustainable. Proof that I could turn nothing into something, then keep pushing and pushing to see what happens. But momentum doesn't come with a steering wheel (or a brake). It doesn't care where it's taking you. Its only job is to go, and left unchecked, it can throw you in a ditch just as easily as it can launch you into space.

What I needed wasn't more speed. It was direction.

I started Career Benders largely out of necessity, but it was also built upon the confidence that I could do it, paired with a true desire to help people. The growth was organic and, in some ways, unexpected, which put me at an interesting crossroads when deciding how to carry my momentum into the future. That momentum also included *No More Mondays* Podcast, which I had somehow managed to launch among the chaos of overwork. The goal? Inspire others through conversations with people who actually like what they do for work.

At first, I'll admit, it was one more thing on the pile, but the podcast quickly became a lifeline of a different kind. Week after week, I was having conversations with people who had built fulfilling careers and meaningful lives.

The common denominator?

Values.

Alignment.

Purpose.

Those conversations weren't just for my listeners; they were for me. First of all, they helped me see that I needed a clearer and more values-driven way to work my business. I needed to think about impact, not just outcomes, and as strange as it sounds, my own podcast helped me lean into the truths that make me the coach and entrepreneur I am today.

More importantly, hosting a podcast dared me to be seen again, this time not as a résumé writer or even "just" a business owner, but as someone who had something to say about how we work and live.

No More Mondays helped me find my voice while building a community of people I would have never met otherwise. I'm grateful for them, the support they still offer me today, and even more so, the wisdom they give to the people on the other end of the airwaves — and to me.

This is one of the reasons I included companion episodes in this book. I hope they impact you as much as they have me.

What started as the goal to inspire others turned out to be an even better mirror, and the reflection helped me realize that I didn't just need to change the pace. I needed to identify the purpose behind it.

For me, that meant going back to my values.

Not the what-do-I-plaster-on-the-website-to-look-human kind of values, but the ones that actually guide how we show up, even when nobody's looking.

I still remember identifying my first set of core values during one of my Denver runs, sitting in Allegro Coffee shop on Tennyson (sadly, it's no longer there), a place I always found both comforting and inspiring. I loved it so much that I even had a brand photo shoot in its perfectly hipster-meets-old-manufacturing vibe.

August 24, 2025

Midweek Momentum vs. The Sunday Scaries

After nearly 200 conversations, one theme rises above them all: values.

Every guest who's built something meaningful, whether a thriving career, a scalable business, or a purposeful life, started with clarity on what matters most.

Core values aren't a checkbox exercise; they're the compass that simplifies hard choices, anchors us in tough times, and points us toward alignment we'd never find otherwise.

Lesson: When we lead from our values, we don't just work better, we live better.

*Just a girl in a hipster coffee shop,
identifying her core values.*

My values: *fun, intelligent, confident, direct, inspiring,
and approachable.*

Those words became my compass. They didn't tell me exactly what to do next, but they provided a way to measure whether I was on the right track. Over time, they've evolved, but they're still not far off from that scrappy coffee-shop list that became the new foundation upon which Career Benders would grow, inspire, and influence.

When I finally started aligning life and work with those values instead of falling victim to the hustle, something changed. The need for redemption, the urge to prove I wasn't the series of mistakes that plagued our lives just a few years prior, and the frantic energy I was holding onto gave way to something stronger and more meaningful.

A purpose: To inspire confident professionals.

That platform became the foundation I built upon for years, creating something so impactful to others that it has left me forever changed. Eventually, the growth I experienced through Career Benders would help me springboard into an even more important mission and purpose than I ever thought I'd be worthy of, but we'll get to that in Chapter Twelve.

Here's what I've learned since those days in Allegro with too much coffee and not enough sleep: purpose doesn't just happen. It's not a lightning bolt or a neat tagline that suddenly shows up to tell you why you've been placed on this Earth.

That's why values matter so much.

Purpose is cultivated, discovered, and built, brick by brick, on the values we choose to honor and the direction we're willing to follow.

Values don't hand you a map on how to navigate every twist and turn, but they make sure you're at least heading in the right direction — for you.

When I drifted off course in the early Career Benders days, it wasn't because I lacked ambition or clarity; it was because

I wasn't measuring my choices against the things that were most important to me. I hadn't defined my course to begin with. I lacked what became my wayfinders: fun, intelligence, confidence, directness, inspiration, and approachability.

Values are very popular in the coaching world, and for good reason. Like many clichés in this world, they're clichés for a reason, and it's because they're usually true.

A day doesn't go by that I don't see the importance of values in my life, and in others. Whether it's the foundation for a decision to be made or resolving friction, values are usually the name of the game.

Values are not marketing fluff.
They're operating instructions.

They don't have to sound sexy;
they have to feel true to you.

When you use them, even the most
complex decisions become simpler.

When we let values guide us, purpose begins to take shape, not as a single "aha" moment, but as a pattern that emerges over time. That's why purpose isn't about speed; it's about direction.

Hard work with a purpose equals progress.

Growth for growth's sake will eat us alive, but growth aligned with values? That's the kind that creates impact without destroying the person behind it. It's sustainable. It's energizing. It's lasting.

I was never one to think much about the legacy I'd leave behind when I turn to dust, especially since we don't have children, but tapping into my purpose inspired me to want to extend my impact as far, wide, and as long as possible.

No matter how big or small your purpose may be, I hope you're on the journey to find it. Maybe you'll impact millions. Maybe it'll be one person. There's no purpose too big or too small, because even if it is a single human on this earth, to that one person, you will change the entire world. I don't know about you, but I think that will feel like a life well-lived.

Wondering where to start?

If you're thinking, "dang, I've successfully avoided this whole mission, purpose, alignment stuff for thirty-nine years," I get it. This can be just as daunting as the overwhelm we talked about in Chapter One. That said, it can also be a catalyst to the change you seek, so I'll offer a simple framework you can use to get the wheels spinning.

Luckily, it works whether you're building a business, leading a team, or just figuring out what's next in life, so get out that journal and get to work:

September 7, 2024

Harvest This Crop of Sunday Scaries Solutions 🌑

Do you work to cultivate a growth mindset? Focusing on abundance and growth versus scarcity and fear requires more effort than you think.

Whether it's your business, your career, or your life, patience, commitment, and positivity will take you far – that's where we tap into our full potential and bring our purpose into the world.

💡 Lesson: Choose to see the bright side; what is possible instead of what is not.

Compass (Values): What matters most to you? What words actually describe how you want to show up? What do you want people to say about you when you're not in the room?

Direction (Purpose): Based on those values, where do you want to focus your energy? Who do you want to help? How do you want to help them? What change do you want to be part of?

Pace (Sustainable Growth): How will you make progress without burning out? What boundaries, systems, or support do you need to protect your energy?

Bonus: you can download a handy-dandy Core Values worksheet at ***scarygoodread.com/values.***

These aren't questions you should expect yourself to answer by the time you finish that cup of coffee. This is a reflective, leave it, reflect some more, let it marinate kind of situation that will hopefully help you find meaning and stave off burnout. Without living in a bus.

Many entrepreneurs, myself included, detour through years of rock bottom to figure out the direction we should have been heading all along. I'm hoping this exercise (and this book) helps you head yourself off at the pass.

There's a level of clarity that comes from knowing and honoring our values. They're non-negotiables. The checklist. Values point us in the right direction and help us know what turns to take when we reach a crossroads. Purpose is what keeps us going, no matter what roadblocks show up along the way.

As Simon Sinek would say, it is our *why*.

Clarity doesn't necessarily mean certainty. It means intention, and knowing the purpose (the *why*) behind that intention is critical to staying the course when the hurricane threatens to sink the entire ship. It's easier to stay connected and committed to something when we know *why* we're doing it, rather than just aimlessly wandering our way through life.

That connection enables us to **start living by design rather than by default.**

Default is reactive. It's autopilot. Busy, in a blur, burnt out.

Design is thoughtful. Intentional. It's reflective, deliberate, and oh-so human.

Choosing design over default requires us to slow down long enough to understand our motivators, align them with our *why*, and cultivate something around those two truths that resembles a life we actually want to experience.

This fast-moving world is never going to slow down. The emails won't stop. The bills won't magically pay themselves. The bar of performance will keep rising higher and higher, but when we're clear on our *why*, we won't get swept up in someone else's version of success.

We get to build our own.

That's what replaced burnout in the bus for me. It wasn't rest — far from it. But, honoring my values and getting clear on the

January 19, 2025

Why Quitting Could Be the Key to Beating Your Sunday Scaries

Ever set a goal just because it sounds good? Or because a friend is doing it?

There's a difference between operating out of your comfort zone and being wildly out of alignment with who you are, which is why it's impossible to stick to a goal because it sounded cool or someone else picked it.

Your life goals should align with your values.

💡 Lesson: What's the _Why_ that keeps you going?

why behind them, when redemption and recovery stopped being the motivators, values got things moving in the right direction.

Values are the compass.
Purpose is the course.

The *why* is the fuel that keeps the fire burning…without burning you out.

The question isn't whether you will move forward.
You will.
Will it be by default — or by design?

No More Mondays Companion Episodes

Career by Design: No Limits, No Regrets with Nikhil Agharkar *(March 3, 2025)*

Stop Drifting: How to Own Your Career, Your Life, and Your Brand with Andy Storch *(November 16, 2025)*

The Vision Starts with You with Lissi Daniels *(October 11, 2023)*

Chapter 7

WE BELONG HERE

The Bittersweet Joy of Coming Home

"Joy is not in things; it is in us."

Richard Wagner

ON JULY 7, 2022, Jim and I stood on the porch of a 1936 log cabin that hadn't been touched since 1983, holding a "Home Sweet Home" sign with Foster, the last of our original fur gang, grinning at our feet. I wore my favorite Lucky Brand Coca-Cola shirt; Jim had on his signature GoPro Games flat brim. Foster's smile seemed like he knew something we didn't.

That memory will forever be imprinted in my mind, and the photo still sits behind me on my office shelf as a reminder of the day that was both surreal and hard-won.

After years of bankruptcy, bus life, and windowless offices, we had realized a dream twenty years in the making.

A home of our own.

Without wheels.

No caption needed. ♡

The house itself looked more like the backup set to *Stranger Things* than a mountain dream home. She was not a looker, but she was ours. No one could take it away or make us move it. I didn't have to ask to paint the walls or get a cat.

For the first time in years, I felt completely present. Safe. Settled.

We were literally and figuratively…home.

Before you get all weepy with me, let me tell you *nothing* about buying this house was straightforward. When all of your income comes from a business you built from scratch, you don't just hop on mortgage rates dot com, plug in your salary, and see what you can afford.

The process was messy, stressful, and nothing short of a miracle. When I first walked into a lender's office in March of 2022, I had no idea if we had a snowball's chance in hell of owning an *actual* home in the valley we'd called home for more than thirty years combined, or if I was destined for a one-bedroom condo in Iowa.

Sorry if that's your dream. It wasn't ours. Not enough mountains. To each their own.

After our fourth winter in the bus, Jim and I were itching for a bit more elbow room and a heating system that required less manual management. Inflation was starting to creep up, the Fed had just implemented its first quarter-point rate hike, so I figured it was time to see where we stood.

To my surprise, we were preapproved for a lot more than I expected…and just enough *not* to afford anything on the market in the post-pandemic, triple-pricing frenzy that is mountain resort real estate.

So, like anyone freshly armed with a preapproval letter, I took to doom-scrolling Zillow. Hourly. Refresh. Refresh. Nothing worth a second look.

Then, one afternoon, I was driving home to the bus from the grocery store, and I passed a small brown cabin with a For Sale sign out front.

That's not on Zillow.

The second I passed it, something in me said, *That's our house.* I remember it vividly; the cool spring air, the barren post-winter grass, the massive tree stump out front, and the gut feeling I couldn't ignore.

Call it a sixth sense. Call it a divine nudge. Call it the same ***knowing*** that told me Colorado was home, and that we shouldn't have signed the paperwork that May day in an attorney's office in Breckenridge.

I just…***knew***.

I tried to put it out of my mind, and by that I mean I checked Zillow obsessively until it appeared several weeks later, a relisting from a contract that had fallen through. It was still listed at a good $100,000 over our budget, but I couldn't shake the feeling that this house was meant to be ours.

I mentioned it to my friend Ashley, our realtor, who smiled and said, "Let's go see it."

Did I mention this house wasn't a looker?

Outdated to the max, complete with once-white carpet gone gray and more styles of paneling than a 1974 lumberyard, it took a certain amount of vision to imagine the tired blank slate becoming "home," but after turning a gutted yellow school bus into A Bus Called Rio, that's exactly what we decided it could be.

In true we-can't-do-anything-the-easy-way fashion, the buying process turned into its own saga. The sellers had dropped the price, and we put in a conservative offer. They countered, but we were still far from anything within an acceptable standard deviation of the pre-approval (or a non-coronary-inducing mortgage payment).

Nope. No deal.

We waited.

Another (agonizing) month went by, and by then, the house had been sitting on the market for nearly two months, an eternity at a time when homes barely lasted two days. When the sellers scheduled an open house (a Hail Mary of their own), we trusted no one would bite.

We were right. The open house came and went, and we swooped back in.

This time, we put in the best offer we could, with a clause promising not to nickel-and-dime them after inspection, a clever move Ashley suggested, betting that the prior contract had collapsed due to the totality of repairs and upgrades needed.

It worked.

Under contract…on the house no one else wanted.

Sounds about right.

I think we're the only new home buyers on the planet who looked at, offered on, and went under contract on a *single* house in the spring of 2022, but that's what happens when there is literally only one option you can "afford" (and it was meant to be).

We were scheduled to close in twenty-eight days.

As small business owners.

Who hadn't filed our taxes…[14]

---

14 Not tax evasion. Just the glamorous world of small business and the annual "fashionably late" filing strategy catching up with us. Thank God for our miracle-worker CPA.

I'll spare you the nitty-gritty of how many miracles had to align, from IRS documents arriving on the last possible day to me feeling like a never-ending document portal, but thanks to an army of people willing to support the mission, we made it happen.

But not without one final pièce de résistance.

We had to paint the house to buy it.

That's a new one for ya, huh? Apparently, FHA loans don't like appraisals that include the words *peeling paint.* Something about old lead laws from the seventies that Ashley had warned us it might come up...

"Well, we'll just paint the house if we have to," we shrugged.

And that's exactly what we did.

Twelve friends, two days, seventeen gallons of paint (paid for by the sellers, thank you very much), and one massive transformation later, our brown cabin was blue, and we were cleared to close in six days.

Again, if you don't think there's someone up there looking out for you...

After years of icy morning coffee (not to be confused with morning iced coffee), blisters from chopping wood, and more big leaps of faith than a cat with nine lives, we finally claimed our own corner of the Roaring Fork Valley.

There isn't a day that goes by that I don't feel like this roof over our heads is both a miracle and a declaration.

We belong here.

And let the DIY games begin! The first thing to go was the carpet. Three minutes after walking through the door, Jim had it rolled up and hauled out, and underneath we found the original hardwood floors, worn but beautiful. And that set the tone.

Over the first few years, every spare ounce of energy that wasn't going into Career Benders went into turning this throwback into our home. We utilized our DIY bus-building skills to gut the kitchen down to the studs and rebuild it from the floorboards up. The once "grandmother's pink tile bathroom" was no more. Trim, paint, fixtures, and endless hours of sanding, staining, and hammering. Every single swing was from one of our arms.

We traded spray foam and plywood for tile saws and floor sanders, but the spirit was the same: build it ourselves, make it our own.

Somewhere in the middle of it all, I carved out my dream office.

First picture of my favorite room.

The corner office.

A room with so much sunlight pouring through the windows that it made up for all the offices closets without them. The room also came with built-ins, which gave me the one thing, yes, the one thing on my "house dream list": a Career Benders blue bookshelf. A little brand-blue paint, and I had the physical manifestation of the business that made the whole thing possible.

We really should have been on HGTV (I'm not sure they could air that much cursing). Step by step, room by room, this log cabin started to look less like a barren, unloved relic and more like a reflection of us. Cozy. Quirky. Inviting. Full of nostalgic heirlooms, storied art, and the type of love that makes a place feel like Christmas all year round.

We had claimed our space.

Every dinner at a real table, every shower longer than seven minutes, and every morning cup of coffee without seeing my breath, in a room that didn't move, made me more present and grateful for what we had accomplished.

And then two months later, we lost Foster.

One week, we were backpacking, and the next…he stopped eating. It turns out, a sudden and merciless heart tumor had formed in his otherwise energetic ten-year-old body. His constant presence and emotional connection to us left a hole so big I'm not sure it'll ever be filled. But I also know, guardian that he was, he saw us safely into this house and thought, "*Okay, they're good now. My job is done.*"

This time, I couldn't run from it. The distractions of con-current life disasters didn't numb me. I couldn't avoid being present to the loss.

Comfort during the bad days.   Love. Just love.

If you've similarly chosen pets over kids, you know, these aren't "just animals." They're family, and losing Foster was one of the hardest losses I've ever experienced. He was more special than the word special can convey, a dog that even dog-haters loved. He sat in between Jim and me, always, a Foster sandwich we used to call it, his little eyes peering into our souls and knowing every word we were saying. He was so emotionally connected to us that it was like having another human around. He would have been a great therapy dog.

It might seem like a strange thing to say, but even in the potency of his loss, I felt joy — joy in what he gave us, joy in the memories, joy in the fact that he carried us through a brutal chapter and left us right where we were supposed to be. I will always be grateful for that. So grateful.

And there we were once again. Just Jim and me...and Tacocat.

Oh, that's right. You haven't met Taco: the oversized road-trip souvenir we scooped up in Kansas City a year earlier. He and Foster had been the best of friends, break-the-internet cute in the way only a senior pittie and a kitten can be.

Best of friends in a bus.

They say you don't find cats; cats find you, and Taco proved that to be true. He became the bridge we didn't know we'd need to grieve Foster until the next chapter revealed itself.

August 28, 2022

Teach Your Sunday Scaries a Lesson!

Give and get love from a furry friend! Animals are proven to lower our stress, so this is a kind of love we can all benefit from. Even if you don't have one of your own to lighten the mood, you can foster a dog, take a shelter pet for a walk, or give a kitty some love at a local adoption event.

Lesson: My dog, Foster, will be happy that you gave a friend of his a scratch behind the ears.

Furry Friends Ease Your Sunday Scaries

The best paths aren't always planned. I know what Tim was thinking that day in the park when I said, "Honey, I hear an animal crying...and I think it's a cat."

He pretty much knew right away that we had likely just acquired a kitten, especially when he so valiantly climbed down a hill in the brush to discover what was an adorable little orange kitten (my fave).

An accidental pet, a road trip, or a surprise job opportunity – don't be afraid to explore things that come out of the blue.

💡 Lesson: The best things in life come when we least expect them!

That grief was sharp and so painful, but it impacted me differently than it had with Raia or Jax. The weight of bankruptcy, homelessness, and survival had made me too numb to really feel it. And while this time I was steadier and more focused on the grief, the home we had provided the grounding to carry it.

If that makes no sense to you, then think about it this way: ever been to a funeral?

Everyone is simultaneously grieving the loss of a loved one while delighting in the joy of memories, togetherness, and love. That's the incredible thing about grief and joy; they aren't opposite. They sit at the same table.

Grief makes sure we don't skip the parts that matter, and joy gives us the strength to keep moving through the sadness.

That truth changed how I showed up. I'm not sure why, but I think it goes back to something similar that had happened long ago when I left that little apartment on French Street.

Closure.

Foster was the last link to the life Jim and I had before; he was the last piece of a puzzle that we had been able to disassemble and put away. It was bittersweet to close that chapter, but in hindsight, I think that's what happened the day we said goodbye to Foster in the quiet of our living room.

And in that goodbye, I was also somehow able to say hello. I started saying yes. I said no to playing small and yes to opportunities. Yes to rooms I used to stand outside of, waiting for permission to enter. Yes to conferences, panels, and workshops, and most importantly, yes to the stage.

Did you know that nearly 75 percent of the global population is afraid of public speaking?

Not me. Never.

I revel in it. I love the spotlight, not for the attention, but for the chance to connect. To educate. To delight and impact at scale. To stand in front of a room and feel the energy shift when an idea lands. Don't ask me to go up on stage and act for a hot second. But present in full, 100 percent authentic glory?

I'm joyously game.

The stage brought me back to something I'd forgotten while in the grind of survival, shame, and staying small. I'm good at this. I belong here. And when I leaned into that joy, the opportunities didn't just add up, they multiplied. The rooms got bigger, the stages got brighter, and the chance to use my voice grew louder,

With each yes, my world expanded, and I don't mean the metaphorical kind. I mean, like legit. It expanded my world.

It carried us across the pond.

What had started as an executive coaching engagement turned into a "think outside the box" speaking invite. In France. And that turned into Jim's bucket-list trip to a country he's been fascinated with since he was barely a teenager, long before he became a wine geek.

For both of us, it was our first adventure overseas, and we got to experience it *together*.

Paris, Mont-Saint-Michel, and Avignon by way of public speaking?

December 9, 2024

Au Revoir, Sunday Scaries 🇫🇷

Tim has been dreaming of a trip to France since he was a teenager. He's finally getting to use his college-era language skills (French major) and to see firsthand what he fell in love with as a sommelier.

It's taken 41 years and 357 days (did I mention we get to celebrate both of our birthdays here?!) for him to check the number one item off his bucket list. And I got to give it to him.

💡 Lesson: The best things in life are worth the wait. 🩶

Twist my arm.

France was pure joy. The kind of kid-like, eyes-wide joy that makes you forget you're a grown adult with bills and responsibilities. Both of our December birthdays were celebrated on the trip, Christmas markets twinkling in every square, and not a single American tourist in sight. We had the country (and the *vin chaud*) practically to ourselves.

We spent our days wandering ruins and our nights indulging in everything Jim's sommelier heart could desire, from Michelin Star restaurants to calling oysters and frites dinner at the Marché de Noël in Tours. We were in heaven, right down to the fondue in Geneva I could have bathed in.

Somewhere between the Louvre and Châteauneuf-du-Pape, I realized *this is what it feels like to be alive in your own story.*

Call it traveling or call it joyful presence. We were living.

This might be one of our biggest life milestones, but that isn't why this was living. This was living because of how we approached it, how we claimed the space, and how we immersed ourselves in every moment. It was love, adventure, togetherness, and joy wrapped up into one beautiful Champagne toast. *How very Callen.*

Space and presence aren't so much about signing mortgage papers or gutting a kitchen.

They're about deciding we belong, in rooms, on stages, or in conversations where our instinct might be to stand outside and

Au Revoir!

Pont du Gard, France.

First vineyard visit in Chateauneuf-du-Pape, Chateau Fortia.

wait for an invitation. Too often, we treat space like something we have to earn: *when I'm more qualified, when I've achieved more, when someone else says I can.*

I call bullsh*t on that script, and you should, too.

The moment we say, *I'm here. I'm enough. I belong*; we assume the power. We take control. We stop outsourcing our worth to job titles, gatekeepers, or the peanut gallery of haters who always seem to have something to say.

From that place, we see things differently. Perspectives shift. Instead of "Why is this happening **to** me?" we can ask: "How is this happening **for** me?"

This is why we have to stop diminishing ourselves or contorting to fit in the box. Why we have to walk into that scary room. Raise our hand when we feel underqualified. Offer $80,000 under asking on the house. Take the speaking gig that's so far out of our league. Fill that seat at the table before we're "ready."

Saying yes is how we step into the space that was ours to take all along, and more importantly, it's how we make space for others, too.

But that's just the start.

Presence is what allows us to experience the joy of that space we've claimed. Are we protected from pain? Of course not. We're never going to be bubble-wrapped against hard things and hard times, but being present keeps us awake to what's happening in front of us: the love, the humanity, the small moments that get us through.

That is the beauty of the human experience.

While none of this eliminates the Sunday Scaries completely, it does stop them from spiraling out of control. Being present, choosing to find the good, realizing that being miserable in a miserable situation gets us nowhere — this is what keeps us from getting complacent.

Instead of letting Monday ruin our Sundays, we can pause, breathe, and remember: this is just one moment. We get to choose how we meet it.

How many of our Sunday Scaries come from exactly this? We let anxiety about tomorrow steal joy from today. We run a hundred mental tabs in the background, but forget to notice the glass of wine in our hand or the person sitting next to us on the couch. Presence doesn't erase the dread, but it interrupts the pattern. It snaps us back into reality long enough to remember and acknowledge what's good…**right now.**

And then there's joy. Not happiness. Not a smile. Not being glad. Sheer, unabashed, feel it in our bones *joy*.

No one gets to steal it from us.

Not the haters.

Not the people rooting for us to fail.

Not the boss who can't see our worth.

Other people's opinions say more about *them* than they ever will about *us*. They can take the job, the title, the business, even the house, but there's one thing they can't touch: our joy.

Joy is a choice.

April 16, 2025

Don't Be Crabby About the Sunday Scaries

Reality is rarely as bad as we make it out to be in our minds. Most of what we dread never comes true, yet we're really good at assuming the worst possible scenario all the time!

When your brain starts racing, stop and ask yourself: What if this "catastrophe" actually does happen? Would it really be the end of the world or just something I'd handle and move on from?

💡 Lesson: Notice when your brain starts making a movie out of Monday — and pause the drama.

It's not a finish line we cross when things finally calm down. It's not "someday when I've made it." Joy is perspective. It's choosing to see opportunities in front of us instead of getting stuck inside our circumstances.

That doesn't mean we sugarcoat, ignore hard things, or slather on toxic positivity when things are falling apart. It means we stay open enough to notice joy alongside grief, stress, and uncertainty.

Joy is a state of being, not the destination. It exists less in milestones and more in moments:

Vin chaud at a Christmas market.
Fondue in Geneva.
Standing on a stage with a room of leaders leaning in.
Coffee in a kitchen that doesn't move.
Holding a dog's collar long after he's gone.

Claiming space. Staying present. Choosing joy.

These aren't luxuries. They're resources that are always within reach. They're the antidotes to dread, overwhelm, and fear. They're what keep us from living by default and remind us to live by design. That's so much more than survival.

Claiming space. Staying present. Choosing joy.
The kryptonite to the Sunday Scaries.

No More Mondays Companion Episodes

How to Be Unforgettable, Without a Stage or Spotlight with Phil Mershon *(June 23, 2025)*

Deliberate Evolution: Burnout, Balance & The Ecology of Leadership with Dan Capello *(September 8, 2025)*

How Curiosity and Authenticity Fuel Entrepreneurship with Alyssa Nolte *(September 15, 2025)*

Chapter 8

PLAY IS POWER

Clip-In for the Secret to Sanity

"We don't stop playing because we grow old;
we grow old because we stop playing."

George Bernard Shaw

A MONTH OR two after we started dating, Jim took me on my first mountain bike ride.

I had a bubble-gum pink hardtail "mountain bike" I'd bought for 300 bucks at REI, the kind you ride on bike paths in Breck when you're single, broke, and just trying to be outdoorsy enough to pass. Jim, of course, was (and still is) an avid mountain biker, so his excitement at the idea that I, too, was a "mountain biker" ran away with him.

He jacked up my seat, threw clipless pedals on the bike, and marched me straight to Prince Creek, a popular area I recall having pencil-thin, single-track trails and a climb from hell up a 4WD road that might as well have been as steep as Everest, as far as I was concerned.

The infamous bubble gum pink bike;
if only I had paid to have this book printed in color.

So. Many. Tears.

If you're familiar with mountain biking, you can see the bruises materializing in real time. If you're not a mountain biker, I'll just get to the spoiler alert: I didn't get on a mountain bike again…for thirteen years.

Thirteen stolen years, if you ask me.

I like to tease Jim about how he robbed me of so much time in the saddle, when, if I'm honest, there's a good chance I likely wouldn't have enjoyed it nearly as much then as I do now. I wasn't fit enough to progress the way I've been able to, nor did I have the confidence (or the quads) I've built since. But still… thirteen years!

What changed? CrossFit.

Spinning on the Assault bike had become one of my favorite forms of torture in the gym, and since CrossFit conditions your body to do hard things just as much as it conditions your mind, I started thinking about riding a bike outside again.

The friends I'd made at the gym weren't just training buddies. They were enablers — and cyclists — and eventually, they talked me into taking my second first ride.

I was 42.8 years old. Back in the saddle...at Prince Creek.

Things went a little differently this time. Instead of bruised thighs, tears for days, and a man I somehow still decided to marry, these women empowered me. I was emboldened. And *hooked*.

Jim was shocked when I got home and told him I liked that one ride so much (four hours, for the record; my Strava[15] personal best on that segment is now about sixty-six minutes) that I wanted to get my own bike.

And the owner of a used bike I became, courtesy of Facebook Marketplace and a fourteen-year-old kid who had outgrown his Kona. Yet again, there are perks to being five-one. I hung on to that bike just long enough to confirm I was truly a mountain biker (no air quotes needed), and then upgraded to a full carbon Santa Cruz Tall Boy the following spring. She is, sorry Jim, the love of my life. She also now has clipless pedals.

Being a gear whore is an occupational hazard in mountain life, especially when there are two of you. I mentioned the REI annex in our basement, right?

---

15 Strava: a social network for endurance nerds. If you didn't record, did it even happen? (Asking for a friend.)

Me in my (now) natural habitat.

When we lived in the bus, we had a storage unit that I used to joke was full of outdoor gear and three pieces of heirloom furniture. Turns out, I wasn't really kidding, a reality that revealed itself when we emptied the storage unit and moved into the house.

One night, Jim popped an edible, and several hours of weed-enabled ADHD hyperfocus later, he turned a basement room into a perfectly organized outdoor mecca that rivals just about any retail store. It's full of camping gear, snowboard equipment, SUPs,[16] and skis.

Yes, skis.

---

16 SUP: stand-up paddleboard. You might remember it from an earlier mention where Jim convinced me to test my buoyancy in a Class III rapid.

Up to this point, I had been strictly a snowboarder. A knuckle-dragger, as some would say. If you recall, it's the hobby I picked up when I moved to Boston after college, the reason I moved to Colorado, and therefore, essentially the impetus for this entire book. Who knew a sport could set so many life changes in motion!?

Somewhere around forty-one, though, a switch flipped. I don't know if it was confidence, curiosity, or a midlife growth spurt, but suddenly I wanted to try new things. To take my mountain-girl game to the next level. The foray into mountain biking was actually the second manifestation of my newfound boldness. The winter before, I decided snowboarding wasn't cutting it anymore, and it was time to start the learning curve over again.

It was time to learn how to ski.

That Valentine's Day, Jim and I went on what might be the most "us" date of all time: my first attempt at skiing in over twenty years. I had tried it once in college and promptly decided I didn't like the feeling of my legs being ripped from my body.

Now, I had grand visions. Thinking snowboarding would make for a seamless transition, I imagined carving gracefully down green runs, just as I had seen Jim do when he converted from snowboarding to skiing earlier that very season. Instead, I spent the day getting passed by five-year-olds in puffy coats.

By Sunday night, I could barely sit down to pee. By Monday morning, I was hobbling through CrossFit, as if I'd been hit by

December 4, 2023

Ski Past the Sunday Scaries: Slope-Smart Tips to Improve Your Week

---

Balance is critical on skis and in life. Just as there's a sweet spot to balancing on your skis to put them on edge, you have a sweet spot to stay healthy in your work-life balance.

💡 *Lesson: Find it. Embrace it. Protect it at all costs!*

a truck, in what was a very special kind of struggle-bus workout. By Friday, I was ready to go back.

Welcome to Type II fun, y'all!

I'm not sure there is a better example of the power of play than Type II fun, an art we mountain folk have mastered. In case you're unfamiliar, let me bring you up to speed.

Type I fun is fun while you're doing it. Ice cream on a hot day, a good concert, floating down the river with a beverage in hand. Easy, enjoyable, memorable.

Type II fun doesn't necessarily feel great in the moment. It's painful, exhausting, sometimes terrifying, and often begs the question, *Why am I putting myself through this?* Until it's over, when your memory seemingly erases itself, and you're ready to go in.

Exhilaration!

Funny how that one word makes you forget everything — how bad it hurt, how bad *you* hurt — you can't wait to do it again. You can't stop talking about it, thinking about it, and you find yourself wanting to get better and better, so the bar of Type II fun keeps rising. Mountain biking, skiing, summiting big peaks, and even CrossFit. They're all some variety of Type II fun. Fly fishing even feels like an adventure when you're waist-deep in a frosty river trying to find traction on slimy rocks.

That's not to say you have to be into scraped-up knees, bloody elbows, and unintentional swims in chest waders to take advantage of the power of play. Music, gardening, reading a book, board games, dancing in your kitchen…anything that pulls you out of autopilot and drops you into a present, kid-like state will do.

Catch of the day.

Play is power because it gives us a release.

We prove to ourselves that we can do hard things with our bodies, and that confidence translates to our minds. It fuels resilience, sparks creativity (my VA[17] swears all my best *Sunday Scaries* emails come on the heels of a great ride), and builds connection,

17 Virtual assistant (sometimes called remote assistant): in this case, the person who helped push many a newsletter out each week for years. Hi, Kristen.

to ourselves, to each other, and if you're lucky, to the trail or mountain underneath your feet.

We've been conditioned to treat play like it's a kids-only game. Once we reach adulthood, it becomes an extra. A nice-to-have. A reward.

Play is not a reward we earn once we've checked enough boxes, hit enough milestones, or collapsed into a weekend.

Play is a requirement.

Think about it: how many times have you dangled fun in front of yourself as a carrot?

When I finish this project, I'll take a trip.
When I hit this goal, then I'll go back to the gym.
When things calm down, then I'll make time for friends.

Hard truth: "then" never comes. There's always another project, another goal, another reason to keep kicking the can down the road, so I'm going to suggest playing hard *now*.

The more we build play into our lives, the more capacity we have to handle the hard stuff. It gives us margin. It restores our energy, resets our perspective, and reminds us we're more than just what we produce.

This is why play has to move from optional to nonnegotiable.

For me, it's as simple as a morning coffee walk with Steve. (Confused? No, I didn't ditch Jim after Chapter Five, but I did get us a dog. More on that in a few.) It's not fancy, and it's not always Type II fun, but it's play built into the

May 25, 2025

Lighten Up the Summer Sunday Scaries

A Tuesday night bike ride with my friend Laurel was just that, a Tuesday night bike ride. 😁

This might seem like a strange thing to those of you who don't look at a mountain bike trail out of your window every day, but this is what "maximizing access" to the things you love affords you.

A not-so-epic bike ride with no personal records, no big story, and no new trail exploration. Just a local favorite that left the night better than we started.

💡 *Lesson: Adventure doesn't have to be grand to be good.*

day. A cup of coffee, some fresh air, my favorite pooch, and the charm of our neighborhood streets. Even better if we can play hooky for a quick ride on our backyard trail. Regardless, this stuff sets the tone for the day better than any to-do list ever could.

Of course, play doesn't always come easy, or without its downsides.

In December of 2023, Jim blew out his ACL and meniscus during opening day at Aspen Highlands. For a guy whose love language is Type II fun, the injury proved to be more than just a physical setback. It was an identity crisis triggered by the temporary loss of spontaneity, adventure, and play.

No biking. No skiing. No river SUP. No mushroom-foraging. No quick hikes or trail runs. For almost a year. Naturally, upon finding out that Jim would be on reduced activity, I did the most logical thing I could think of.

I got us a dog.

In one of my most idiotic yet inspired moments, I decided the best way to help a man who couldn't walk, in the middle of winter, on the day before his birthday, was to get him a puppy. Or, in Jim's words: I got "the cripple" a dog. (I stand by the decision.)

What was a well-intentioned, but maybe poorly thought-out, recovery companion for Jim became an "I got myself a Jim-blew-out-his-knee recovery gift." And before we knew it, Steve exploded into our lives like a furry hand grenade.

Ya know, sometimes I think that was how it was meant to be.

Welcome home, baby Steve!

He had more energy than all of our previous furkids combined. In the evenings, when all I wanted to do was crash on the couch where Jim had become a permanent fixture, Steve would pace laps around us. Frozen peanut butter and a dog puzzle would last twenty minutes, and the pacing would begin once more.

This dog had one-thousand percent energy and zero respect for the fact that his new home included exactly one able-bodied human, so my tertiary mission, after caregiver and breadwin-

May 16, 2024

Some Puppy Love to Fight Your Sunday Scaries

There really is nothing like the love of an animal, especially one you rescue.

Steve is still getting used to a world full of humans after starting life on a reservation. Knowing we are giving him a better life fills my soul every day.

I know people choose dog breeds for many different reasons, but next time you're thinking about getting a dog, consider the impact your loving home could have on a rescue.

💡 Lesson: Go pet a furry friend!

ner, became walks, hikes, training, and "How can I get as much energy out of this dog as possible ?"

His giant ears, ridiculous personality, and insatiable energy kept me on my toes and both of us laughing, forcing Jim just a tiny bit out of his wallow of self-pity as we found new ways to play.

The thing about play is that it's not just physical.

It's mental, emotional, even spiritual.

Play is not just for kids. It's a powerful tool for adults to regulate emotions, recover from burnout, and reconnect with creativity.[18] Research shows that adults who regularly engage in play, whether through sports, music, hobbies, or outdoor adventures, report lower stress, higher resilience, and better problem-solving skills.

Play also shapes who we are. We talked back in Chapter Five about how identity isn't just the titles we hold, but the things that light us up. Play is part of that equation. When Jim jokingly responds to "So what do you do?" with "I ski in the winter and bike in the summer," he's not just talking about hobbies. He's naming who he is at his core. That's the kind of identity that endures no matter what happens to our résumés or roles.

It also provides consistency when circumstances change. Play provides a grounding, even when life gets sidelined by a knee

18 Ontario Psychological Association, "Playfulness and Play for Adults," 2025; *Healthy Minds Monthly Poll*, American Psychiatric Association, 2023; National Institute for Play. "Go play outside" wasn't just a way for Mom to get us out of her hair.

injury, a hard season, or just the everyday grind. It reminds us that joy isn't something we wait for; it's something we practice.

When we push our bodies up a climb, fly down a hill, or push through a workout we swore we couldn't finish, the confidence doesn't stay on the trail or in the gym. It follows us into meetings, relationships, decisions, and risks. It gives us a release. It lets us laugh at ourselves, shake off the heaviness, and reset our nervous systems so we don't burn out in the process of "doing it all."

And it sparks creativity. Ask any rider, runner, or artist where their best ideas come from. Newsflash: it's usually not hunched over a desk. It's in motion. It's in flow. In the shower. On the road. Out in nature. At a piano. With a paintbrush.

Of course, play builds connection, too. To ourselves. To each other. To the mountains and rivers and neighborhoods that shape us. Sometimes, even to a goofy puppy with giant ears who forces you to get off the couch and back into the world.

This is why play can't sit in the "optional" category, waiting for when we've earned it.

It's power. It's presence. It's resilience.

It's not frivolous. It's essential.

And when we treat it that way, as a nonnegotiable, as a resource already within reach, we don't just stay alive. We come alive.

Consider this your invitation to play.

No More Mondays Companion Episodes

Beat the Burnout: Living Stoked with Sarah Bettman *(February 28, 2024)*

A Chat with Our Favorite Predictor of Powder: Joel Gratz on Turning a Passion into a Business *(April 25, 2023)*

Fueling the Entrepreneurial Engine: The Power of Health and Wellness with Mark Gray *(November 18, 2024)*

From Burnout to Brilliance: How Creativity and Fun Can Transform Work and Life with Mike Brennan *(January 27, 2025)*

Chapter 9

WHERE FRUIT TREES GROW

The Biology of Belonging

"Alone, we can do so little; together, we can do so much."

Helen Keller

I WAS ABOUT five years old. I had climbed up on the kitchen counter to get the peanut butter and jelly out of the cabinet to make myself a sandwich…at age *five*. From that vantage, which probably doubled my height at the time, I could see down the hall and into my parents' bedroom.

My mom was in bed, going through the stacks and stacks of cards she had received from friends, church members, and loved ones, while a mechanized sleeve that went up to her thigh pulsed on and off. Air in. Air out. Air in. Air out. Compression therapy before it was cool.

I've celebrated just about every holiday, life milestone, and birthday in a hospital. One of those birthdays, my fifth, also happened to be the day my mom hemorrhaged eleven pints of blood due to stomach ulcers the size of a man's fist. Quick science lesson: the body only holds twelve pints of blood. It was one of her many near misses with death, although I was too young to remember many of the specifics of that particular instance.

What has been recounted to me is that after months in an ICU most people don't leave alive, experimental treatment after experimental treatment, and thousand-milligram doses of prednisone, she made it. She was diagnosed with a rare-at-the-time autoimmune disease (Wegener's; it isn't called that anymore because, apparently, he was a Nazi), and spent decades battling lung disease, vasculitis (hence the compression sleeve), and kidney disease on top of early-onset rheumatoid arthritis.

When I was in eighth grade, I remember Dad coming into my history class to pull me out. They had gone to a doctor's appointment and found out Mom was no longer in remission. It was back, but that bout wasn't nearly as seared into my brain as the one in 2007 when her kidneys shut down six months before her scheduled live-donor transplant.

I was living in Boston at the time. No daughter wants that panicked 5 a.m. voicemail from Dad: "Ang, you'd better fly home. Now."

She would eventually end up having that transplant in the summer of 2008. I can still see her being rolled out of the elevator after our agonizing twelve-hour hangout in the surgery waiting room. There was Soni, arms waving overhead, a big smile on her face, celebrating a prize more valuable than the MVP's trip to Disney World after the Super Bowl.

In short: I'm lucky she's still here. Lucky I have wedding photos with her by my side. Lucky for every single emoji heart she leaves on my business posts. (She may have cornered the market on heart emojis before they were cool, too; she has always signed her name, Soni, with a heart over the i.)

She's listened to every episode of *No More Mondays*, including the reruns, when she'll text me, "Hey, this person sounds familiar…" She's been my biggest fan, even when I wasn't really worth following. And if I ever forget where I come from, I look at Soni and Floyd and see it: Dad's brains, easy charm, and command of a room; Mom's hospitality, need to serve, and, you guessed it, love of people.

You can thank both of them for that chapter on resilience.

That's the kind of community I was born into: cards, casseroles, phone calls, faith, and compassion. Money may have been tight (and then some), but the love I felt made up for it. It's the template I carried forward, even from thousands of miles away.

Not everyone is fortunate enough to have that kind of start, and even when we do, life eventually requires us to build our own communities. That early lesson in what it means to show up for people stayed with me, even as I ventured further from the nest.

In fact, the further I went, and the longer I've been away from "home," the more I've realized how important it is to find connection and create a circle of people whom we care about

May 12, 2025

Sunday Scaries According to Soni (aka MOM!)

We call my mom the Hallmark lady because she is known for sending a card for any and all occasions.

There's something magical about handwritten notes. They say, "I cared enough to do more than text or email," and I think they're appreciated more now than ever due to these easy technological alternatives.

💡 Lesson: Who can you send a little snail-mail love to this week?

and trust. Humans still matter, and we're meant to do this thing called life *together*.

One of my first true experiences building community was in college. Growing up in a small farming town in southwestern Pennsylvania didn't breed a lot of like-minded people, and stepping into the diversity of Carnegie Mellon was both eye-opening and thrilling.

People like me. Driven, committed, smart, globally minded, and going places. From my tight-knit civil engineering class to the sisters of Zeta Psi Sigma (later folded into Alpha Chi Omega), I made lifelong bonds there. I may not see or talk to many of them as often as I'd like; it's natural for communication to fade once the weddings are over, but I know without a doubt that if I needed them, they'd show up.

Community comes in layers. And seasons.

There are times when the community feels close, steady, and safe, and others when Jim and I were the only community each other had, left to rebuild the rest from scratch. (We are pros at that whole ground-up thing by now.) The move into the bus, along with the simultaneous upheaval of life, created a strange dichotomy in our community. One night, friends were helping us haphazardly pack boxes for storage; the next, they ghosted us. It was whiplash, plain and simple. The gaps left behind made me hesitant to trust, but they also forced us to get intentional about the people we pedal with, laugh with, and lean on.

Over time, we pieced together new layers. Found people we trust. Let the rest go. Sometimes, it feels like an entirely different onion, but it's a produce section I'm grateful for.

From neighbors who bring us soup during yet another knee surgery recovery to river friends who gather around a campfire and share stories after long days on the water. Landowners willing to rent us space for a bus, who became unexpected quarantine companions and lifelong friends. Coaches who have gone from conference colleagues to coworkers to confidants.

Chosen family is a powerful thing, even if finding friendships in adulthood is different.

We may not have gone through the formative years together, but we're all more self-aware now. We know what matters, and time is one of those things. I'm honored by the people who choose to spend it with us. Every doorstep meal, dog walk, well-timed text, and layer of paint slapped on a house we didn't yet own is more appreciated now than it would have been during life in Chapter One.

Community isn't just something we have;
it's something we build.

There's a well-known African proverb that goes something like: "If you want to go fast, go alone; if you want to go far, go together." I believe that to my core.

September 14, 2025

Get Surgical with Your Sunday Scaries

Recovery isn't solo work. From the neighbors bringing soup, to friends checking in, to the PT team getting Tim mobile again, it takes a village.

 I'm grateful for that village, including the friends who get me out adventuring while my main outdoor buddy is down for the count. In caregiving, it is just as important to take care of yourself as it is the patient.

Lesson: Healing, progress, and big goals all require support. Don't try to do it alone.

And yet, we're living in a time when we're more divided and more distant from each other than we've ever been. Recent studies show that young adults now spend nearly one thousand fewer hours per year face-to-face with people compared to older generations.[19] That's not just math. That's thousands of hours of laughter, hugs, and connection lost over a lifetime.

A thousand hours traded for scrolling, streaming, and sitting behind a screen, convincing ourselves that "likes" equal connection. There. I said it.

When life gets hard, we tend to want to isolate. Pride gets in the way of asking for help, and before we know it, we're left with no option but to swallow even more pride, crush our ego, and reach out for the help that would have saved a whole lot of pain in the first place.

Hiding is about the only thing that feels safe. Putting on a hat and sunglasses and walking through the grocery store, head down, in the hopes you won't see anyone *who knows.*

Ask me how I know.

Asking for help and holding our heads high when the world is crumbling around us is not easy, but it's *easier.* Easier than waiting until things are so hopelessly broken. Easier than carrying the weight of the stress, the secrets, and the shame so long that we lose part of ourselves in the futile effort to go it alone.

That's the paradox of community. We crave it, yet we resist it. We don't want to burden people. To seem needy. To be vul-

---

19 *The Friendship Recession: The Lost Art of Connecting.* Harvard University Happiness Lab, 2025. Somewhere between dial-up and TikTok, we traded dirt under our fingernails for smudges on phone screens.

nerable. But that's exactly when the people who care about us most want to show up.

The funny thing about community is that we all *actually want* to be there for each other. We want to help. That's what community is: people who value each other enough to step in when the time is right.

Why don't we let them?!?

Because we're too self-centered, too proud, or too afraid to let anyone in. But we're not just cutting ourselves off when we do this; we're robbing others of their chance to serve.

I often think about the pioneer days when I think of community. In addition to believing I would have made one hell of a frontierswoman, I also think they had something that we'll never know: genuine connections within the textbook definition of community.

A horse ride was as far as one could go. Circles were small. Living off the land was a shared experience, not because it was nice to give neighbors tomatoes from the eight-foot trellis your husband built in your townie backyard garden, but because it was essential for survival.

I would have been the bread baker if I lived in those days. Hopefully, celiac disease wasn't a thing yet.

Leaning into community means doing things like asking for help, lending a hand, and saying, "Sure, I'll take some leftovers" when offered. It is being gracious. Easy to help and equally as giving in the help. And when we accept that help with honesty and humility, others feel needed, useful, and trusted.

Asking like a greedy opportunist? That's how we end up on a list of the never-ending Meal Trains no one wants to sign up for again. But when we surround ourselves with people who share our values, asking and giving don't feel like transactions. They feel like trust, love, and support.

Generosity compounds.

A ride to the airport turns into a hand with moving boxes. A casserole turns into business advice. A dog walked, a driveway plowed, a porch light left on. Every time we give freely of our time, knowledge, and resources, we're making deposits in what I call the karma bank.

The ROI on that is exponential, but the payoff isn't just favors or traded meals. The real return is transformation.

Community shapes who we are and how we get there. So much of what you've read so far is about discovering yourself: what you value, who you are without titles, how you handle stress, being brave, and how you play. Our inner circle not only enables that discovery but keeps us accountable to it.

They're there to remind us of our best selves when we forget.

Surround yourself with people who cheer you on, hold your feet to the fire, bring a different perspective, challenge you physically, mentally, spiritually, emotionally, and you've got a kickass way to do life.

You don't have to take my word for it, although if you've stuck with me this far, there's a good chance you will anyway. In *Wellbeing: The Five Essential Elements*, Tom Rath and Jim Harter leverage the wealth of Gallup's research to define the five

June 29, 2025

Adulting My Way Out of the Sunday Scaries

We are incredibly blessed; I mean, there is no word strong enough to explain what amazing neighbors we have, and they have become some of our closest friends. Glasses of wine on porches, impromptu dog playdates, bike rides, cookbook trades...and that's just the start.

It turns out that the world opens up when you step away from your computer and head outside.

Lesson: Community finds you if you're visible enough. Who might be looking for you?

elements that determine our quality of life: finance, physical, career, social, and community.

In case it isn't obvious: two of the five are about people (and we can pose a strong argument that the career bucket is a third).

The recovering engineer in me can't help but break this down to a simple formula. At least 40 percent of our overall well-being, satisfaction, and quality of life is directly tied to the people we surround ourselves with, where we live, and the involvement we have in our communities.

I rest my case.

I didn't just learn this theory or buy into data I read in a book. I've lived it from the day I was born, and in the fall of 2023, that came full circle.

My parents made their very first trip to Colorado.

It took over fifteen years to make it happen, no thanks to the many limitations of my mom's lifelong health challenges, but buying our house gave them the push they needed. And by push, I mean...

A road trip.

From Pennsylvania.

Four days, three nights each way, and my dad did every lick of the driving. He still insists Kansas is amazing.[20] We still make fun of him for it.

---

20 There's one in every family.

For two weeks, our house became a home in the truest sense. We played cards at the kitchen table and made farm-to-table dinners from our backyard garden. We took them to the Maroon Bells and Moab, which put Kansas to shame. My mom walked to the post office every day, as if it were her own mini-mountain adventure. She shooed Taco off the counter while she made chicken salad, put her feet up while sitting just out of the sun in

" It's like we're on Mars!" - Dad

Mom and Dad and the
Maroon Bells, September 2023.

September 24, 2023

Parenting Away Your Sunday Scaries

My parents are visiting us in Colorado for the first time since I moved here 15 years ago! In honor of this historic event, and their 45th wedding anniversary, I let them take over the Sunday Scaries.

🌱 Lesson: A good life according to Soni and Floyd is always respecting and listening to each other, meaning what you say, empowering others to spread their wings, not confining growth, always seeking improvement, keeping the faith, and listening to your elders.

the backyard, and treated herself to a haircut at a random salon in Carbondale.

My dad and Jim planted fruit trees in our backyard, and my mom and dad got to be part of one of the most meaningful moments of all: laying Jax, Raia, and Foster's ashes to rest under those trees. Apricot for Jax. Peach for Raia. Cherry for Foster, where a small stone heart reads: *No longer by my side, but forever in my heart.* I read the Rainbow Bridge poem for every single one of those beloved family members, and we stood together, full of tears and gratitude, as the past and the future were woven into our permanent little patch of heaven.

Remembering Foster, and all of our furkids who now live over the Rainbow Bridge.

It wasn't just a visit. It was worlds colliding in the best of ways. The community I was born into finally met the one Jim and I had cultivated together. My parents, the ones who taught me about cards, casseroles, and kindness, were standing in the miraculous backyard of the life we had created, surrounded by neighbors who had gifted us those fruit trees to plant, friends who shared holidays, and the kind of love that makes a place feel like home.

Parents willing to drive four days across the country. Neighbors showing up with a snow shovel when you need it most. Friends who somehow become family along the way.

Life wouldn't be the same without them.
That's the power of community and connection.

No More Mondays Companion Episodes

The Power of Community: Build Connection, Courage, and Freedom with Vincent Pugliese *(April 28, 2025)*

Say Yes: Building Careers and Communities Through Connection with Greg Wasserman *(September 22, 2025)*

Humanizing Communication: How to Speak With People *(Not At Them) with Jason Raitz (October 13, 2025)*

Chapter 10

LEADERSHIP ISN'T A VERB

And Other Things Corporate America Forgot

"If your actions inspire others to dream more, learn more, do more, and become more, you are a leader."

John Quincy Adams

I'VE LOVED LEADERSHIP since I was fifteen years old.

That was the year I was selected as the lone delegate from my high school to attend the Hugh O'Brian Youth Leadership (HOBY) seminar. Honestly, I probably loved leadership from a much earlier age; it does come naturally to me, but this was the first time I was able to define it. To study it. To sit in a room full of similarly extroverted peers, all buzzing with ideas on how to make the world better.

It was so intoxicating that I can still remember the rooms, the people, and the experience *cough cough* thirty years later. I loved HOBY so much that I stayed with them for years, serving as a junior counselor for several seminars after my own, and then joining the HOBY Alumni Boards in both Pennsylvania and Massachusetts after I moved.

By the time high school graduation rolled around, I walked across that stage with leadership oozing out of my bones and bursting at the seams to experience life beyond my small town.

I was one of the speakers at McGuffey High School's Class of '99 graduation. Our school had decided to name a "top three" instead of valedictorians and salutatorians, a very early attempt at the Millennial "everyone gets a trophy" M.O. we've become all too familiar with today. (My dad, who, if you recall, was my math teacher, was furious. Classic Boomer.)

The three of us worked together to develop a collaborative speech inspired by a Ralph Waldo Emerson poem. I had the honor of kicking it off, reciting the first several stanzas of a poem I still love reading in full today:

"To laugh often and much:
To win the respect of intelligent people
and the affection of children,
to earn the appreciation of honest critics
and endure the betrayal of false friends;
to appreciate beauty,
to find the best in others,
to leave the world a bit better,
whether by a healthy child, a garden patch,
or a redeemed social condition;
to know even one life has breathed easier
because you lived.
This is to have succeeded."

Somewhere in my subconscious, I must have taken those words and made them my lifelong personal mantra. If that isn't foreshadowing, even down to the false friends, I don't know what is.

Funny enough, that poem wasn't actually Emerson's at all. It was written by Bessie Anderson Stanley in 1904 for a magazine contest. But thanks to Ann Landers, the misattribution stuck.

Regardless of the author, I believed, and still believe, every word. Even as a bright-eyed teen whose entire world lay ahead of her, I looked at success as something more than the accolades and achievements I had already racked up. I'm not sure I could have articulated this at the time, but I knew success was about making an impact, being present, and leaving people better than you found them.

Man, am I a Gen X-er with Millennial tendencies, or what?

Looking back, it's almost funny how consistent the leadership thread has been. From HOBY and that graduation stage, to keynotes and coaching years later, I've always been a "front of the room" person.

Not because I needed the spotlight, but because I don't know any other way to be.

It's probably no surprise that in the spring of my sophomore year of college, I was chosen as one of six Head Orientation Counselors (HOCs) at Carnegie Mellon University. This was *the* position on campus at the time, a coveted role given only to the leaders and connectors intimately involved in Student Life.

For nine months, we worked with Anne Witchner, the powerhouse behind Student Life, first-year orientation, and my first true mentor, to design Orientation 2001 for the incoming class of 2005.

Bea Diaz, Amber Jackson, Chad Paliotta, Casey Helfrich, Beth Lass, and me.

I can rattle off those names as if it were yesterday (*Hi, I know some of you are reading!*) because we were a unit. Days were spent planning programs, designing events, and shaping the experience of 1,500 incoming students. Nights were spent playing games, hitting the town, and laughing our way through the kind of summer that changes you.

For me, it certainly did.

That summer wasn't just about the logistics of color-coded T-shirts, CD cases adorned with the "Add to the Mix" paint-can theme logo, or the fleece blankets we handed out to the Orientation Counselors as if they were the coolest piece of swag ever created.

It was when I really began to understand that leadership isn't just organizing, delegating, or managing.

Leadership is inspiration.

Shout out to one of our OCs who conveniently posted this picture on Facebook recently. Thanks for the perfectly timed throwback (and photo permission!).

Casey and I had been tasked with training the entire team of orientation counselors (OCs), dozens of our peers who would be on the front lines with the first-year students — a role I had filled the previous summer. Apparently, Anne knew I had natural teaching and training abilities, even all those years ago.

I can still remember the night before the first-year students arrived. We had gathered all of the OCs, probably 200 to 300 of them, into a tent that had been temporarily put up on The Cut (which was our fancy word for the lawn in the middle of campus; nerds cannot be trusted to call anything by a normal name) for a pep rally of sorts.

I found myself giving what I now recognize as my first real motivational speech.

I don't remember exactly what I said, but I remember the feeling. I can put myself back on that stage. See the lights. Feel the energy. The way the room leaned in. The way people laughed and clapped and left ready to give the week everything they had.

This is what I'm meant to do.

My world opened in so many ways that summer. It wasn't just the late nights with my fellow HOCs or the rallying tent full of peers. It was my first real taste of independence — of *self-leadership*.

I flew on an airplane for the first time. Yes, I was almost twenty-one before I boarded a plane, and when I did, I went all the way to San Francisco to visit a friend interning at Apple. Fireworks off the pier on the Fourth of July. A walk along the beach, where I saw sea otters for the first time. Exploring the streets of San Francisco beside people who felt like they belonged to a different universe from my small-town Pennsylvania roots.

It was new geography, yes, but it was also new perspective. I realized that leadership wasn't just confined to where I finished in my graduating class, the title on my campus badge, or the training manuals we wrote. It was about showing up in the world with curiosity, courage, and connection…the same ballsy things that made me climb on a stage in a tent and send 200 college kids out into the night believing they could change the world for a bunch of nervous freshmen.

That was the summer I learned leadership is portable. It's not something we leave behind when the last guest leaves the audience, and novelty T-shirts get folded into a drawer.

Leadership is a *way*. A way of moving through the world. A way of seeing people. A way of holding ourselves accountable to something bigger than ourselves. A way of leaving our mark.

What that young adult could never have known is how sticky leadership would actually be, and eventually it came back to meet me, right there on stage. Public speaking had followed me around throughout most of my career, presenting small workshops and at conferences I was already attending. But the bar raised big-time in 2024, when I was coaching an executive who casually asked, "Do you do any speaking? I need someone to come to a conference and talk about leadership in the AI age."

Cue jaw drop.

And a giant smile.

That keynote, delivered to a room full of marketing leaders, brought me back to HOBY. It brought me back to that tent on The Cut twenty-something years prior. I even had a slide where I shared a good old Class of '99 senior photo of myself, proudly wearing my HOBY sweatshirt. Yes, that experience impacted me so much that I chose that sweatshirt as one of my four signature outfits during the days of pre-cell phone, hard-copy-proof senior photo shoots.

Long live those old school senior photo shoots.

I can't think of a purer display of complete authenticity than printing this in a book for mass publication.

Speaking on that particular stage reminded me not only how much I've always loved leadership, but how alive I feel when I get to inspire people to see their own potential. And it wasn't just that one stage. Since then, I've stood in front of AI leaders talking about humanity, led retreats in France, and helped teams of executives take their collective influence to the next level. And every one of those times, I've walked away just as, if not more inspired, than those I hopefully impacted.

August 25, 2025

From Whiskey to Wisdom: Nashville's Guide to Sounding Off Your Sunday Scaries

---

Sharing your knowledge with someone is a great way to validate your expertise.

For me, standing on that stage and talking about "Leadership in the Age of AI" unlocked a decades-old passion for a topic I didn't realize I should be talking about: leadership. It's also perfect that I get to talk about that during the digital and AI age, as we all know how much I love being a non-robotic, authentic human.

💡 Lesson: What unique gifts and experiences do you have to give away?

Big stages, intimate rooms, coaching circles, or while making my own way through life, the through-line is the same: leadership lights me up. Career Benders, along with the new sister brand, The Modern Coach, have become the places where that love has an outlet, where I turn passion and purpose into practice to bring others forward. Few things have mattered more.

The stage that reignited my love of...the stage... and set so many wheels in motion.

You don't need a stage, a microphone, or a "front of the room" personality to lead.

All of this reminded me that leadership isn't about what we do. It's about who we are. How we impact and inspire. How we meet the demands of leadership in today's world.

Self-awareness. Values. Trust. Connection. Empathy. And yes, even humility.

Celebrating wins when you're in a position of leadership is easy, but it isn't all highlights and applause. I've had plenty of lows as a leader. Hard calls. Missed opportunities. Firing someone for the first time. Hearing "no" for the umpteenth time while struggling to secure funding to keep a drowning business alive. Weathering setbacks, uncertainty, admitting when I was wrong (*what's that saying, eating a little crow?*).

Welcome to the less glamorous side of leadership, where we are tested. And strengthened.

Every leader, which means each one of us, will face a crisis of confidence. Those moments tell us we aren't deserving of the distinction. We're not worthy of the responsibility, but that's also where the irony of leadership reveals itself. Even when we doubt ourselves, something pushes us forward. We may not have all the answers, but innate self-leadership gives us the faith to guide ourselves through the hardest of hard times and the fortitude to pick it all up after it falls apart.

That's a beautiful thing.
Once found, leadership is never completely lost.

It may go dormant, but it doesn't disappear, at least not forever. It may wait, go into hiding, even hibernate for a while, but when it returns, and we choose to step back into our power and purpose, we do so stronger, wiser, and more rooted in who we've become.

Different season, same lesson: the real measure of leadership isn't how brightly we shine. It's how much light we create for those around us.

That's what leadership really is.

Somewhere along the way, we've begun to misunderstand that. We think of, and treat, leadership as if it's a badge of authority rather than a way of living. The title on the door, the corner office, the seat at the head of the table — when treated this way, leadership becomes something different. Something we do at work instead of something carried across all parts of life.

No wonder we feel disconnected from our natural ability to lead ourselves and others. What should be about inspiration, influence, and stewardship has too often been reduced to barking orders. Real leadership — making people feel seen, heard, and capable; putting others before ourselves — has been muddied across all parts of life and work, thanks to corporate America.

The literal definition of leadership, according to our friends at Merriam-Webster, is:

/lee-der-ship/ *noun* — the position or function of a leader, a person who guides or directs a group.

Now, I think it's kinda lame when a word's definition contains part of the word, so our etymological hunt continues to the definition of *lead*.

Lead /lēd/

verb

cause (a person or animal) to go with one by holding them by the hand, a halter, a rope, etc.; be a route or means of access to a particular place or in a particular direction.

noun

the initiative in an action; an example for others to follow.

There it is: *an example for others to follow.*

What is, by nature, an act of kindness, service, and guidance has been confused, maybe even hijacked, by the idea of management. Management, boiled down, is about control: check boxes, keep order, meet deadlines.

But leadership is about taking people with you. Vision. Long-term strategy. The gentle pull of the reins on a horse… (choke up, and the horse rears).

Both leadership and management have their place in life and work. There are seasons when innovation and inspiration are what a team, or our family, needs most. And there are other times when we quite literally need to manage finances, establish structure, and create accountability.

The tricky part is knowing when to do which. Sometimes that's choosing to pause in a tense family conversation instead of snapping back. Others, it's stepping up to run the meeting no one else wants to lead. Maybe it's quietly helping your neighbor shovel their sidewalk before they even ask.

Ordinary, everyday choices like these are where leadership shows up most organically, but when we get the mix wrong, we're out of alignment. Try to manage every moment with control, process, and deadlines…well, say hello to overwhelm. Lead with only vision and inspiration, we float without direction. When the two work together, we feel both effective and fulfilled, and that's often all it takes to keep the Sunday-night anxiety at bay.

Regardless of venue, treating leadership as a *way* rather than a burden lifts the pressure. Life feels lighter, less overwhelming, and more connected. Here's what I've come to believe after years of practicing, failing, coaching, and mentoring on this topic:

Leadership is both innate and learned. Some people are wired for it. Others grow into it. Both are valid, but they show up differently. If it's natural, it flows. If it's learned, it takes practice and energy. But either way, leadership is more active than passive, and it's in *how* we show up, not the title or pretense under which we do so.

Leadership is borrowed. It's not about us. It's about the people who give us their trust, buy into our vision, and decide to follow because they want and choose to, not because they have to. That's why it's sacred. It can be lost as quickly as it's gained, and leadership should never be taken lightly.

Leadership is service. The spotlight might land on you, but the job is moving it onto others. Creating conditions where they succeed, grow, and shine. That's as true in a tent full of college kids as it is in a company, a coaching cohort, or a family.

In summary: leadership isn't situational. It isn't confined to the hours we're at work, or the moments when the microphone is in our hands. Leadership is there when no one is watching. It's present in the smallest of interactions: listening instead of talking, giving trust before it's earned, and modeling the behavior we hope others will carry forward, from clients to colleagues to, you guessed it, kids.

It doesn't matter if you're in a boardroom or at the dinner table. True leadership is how we treat the people at any table, from the colleagues on our teams to the neighbors on our blocks. It isn't a role we clock into and out of. It is a way of being.

Choosing to live with courage, presence, and intention. That's what transforms leadership from a role into a way of life, and it's what makes our lives feel fuller, lighter, and more connected — to ourselves and others.

In doing so, we give others permission to do the same.

No More Mondays Companion Episodes

How Will You Be Great Today? With Andre Young
(May 12, 2025)

Leadership in the Making: The Learn-It-All Advantage with
Damon Lembi *(June 16, 2025)*

From Command to Connection: Modern Leadership with
Christopher Sprague *(September 29, 2025)*

Chapter 11

CONFIDENCE IN ACTION

Measure Once, Cut Anyway

"Inaction breeds doubt and fear. Action
breeds confidence and courage."

Dale Carnegie

"HOW DO YOU know how to do that?" People ask us that all the time.

When Jim and I lived in the bus, conversations about how we transformed a not-level, not-square steel bullet into something we could call a home were as regular as explaining where we went to the bathroom while living in it. (Yes, toilet talk can apparently be a topic for dinner conversation with strangers.)

The DIY didn't stop with the bus. In our *real* house, we started a down-to-the-subfloor kitchen renovation on our first Thanksgiving after moving in. When else would you take a sledgehammer to the counter?

And I'm not talking painting cabinets here, friends. I'm talking video footage of me jackhammering concrete. Running new breakers to the panel, so we could have a dishwasher. Upgrading knob-and-tube wiring to install those "new-fangled" three-prong outlets. That, along with the acrobatics required to fish Romex through the walls of a log cabin, will be a source of pride until the day I die.

Do. Not. Mess with me.

Plumbing in a near-100-year-old house is no less of an undertaking. Nothing is a traditional pipe size, and the materials seem to change every five feet. Let's just say we're lucky to live six minutes from Lowe's.[21] I guess designing their stores all those years has paid off! I've probably single-handedly helped the Lowe's of Glenwood Springs outperform that "crown jewel" the twenty-five-year-old in Chapter One poured herself into.

I have a three-page, single-spaced Word document listing all the improvements we made on the house in just the first three years. From planting fruit trees with Mom and Dad to gutting and refinishing bathrooms entirely on my own (tiling is my love language), we're not afraid to roll up our sleeves — *and try.*

Sure, a background in civil engineering doesn't hurt, nor does Jim's propensity for building model airplanes and Pinewood Derby cars as a kid. But designing detention basins, parking lots, and balsam wood airplanes doesn't exactly translate when the time comes to cut a ten-inch hole in the roof of your bus-house.

So, when someone asks, "How do you know how to do that?" My answer is typically: we learned.

Sometimes the hard way.

We knew we could figure it out on our own (with a little help from YouTube University).

We had the **confidence to act.**

I know where some of this came from. I grew up watching Dad build, renovate, and tinker.

When I was a kid, my mom had a crafting business, and my dad did all the woodwork for her. Cut-out ducks, Christmas

21 Proximity to Lowe's: the DIY version of living next door to Starbucks, equal parts blessing and financial black hole.

trees, and fall pumpkins. We're talking classic '80s craft fair territory here. I can see them, and the giant bandsaw he had in the basement woodshop, as plain as day.

It's a look (No More Mondays, represent!)

The most vivid memory I have of home DIY as a kid is when my dad and Pap turned our unfinished basement into a family room. I was five or six when they built it out, and I can remember peering over their shoulders, asking why *that* wire went *there*.

That space was finished with every bit of 1980s glory you could imagine: burnt-sienna floral couches, off-white paneling with tiny dusty-blue flowers, and a concrete floor painted smoking-room green. The mildewy smell of two, yes two, sets of *Encyclopedia Britannica* will be with me forever, as will the knowledge of how to wire an outlet that I gained sometime around kindergarten.

It could be a limited-resources childhood. Perhaps it's stubborn curiosity. Maybe both. But I've always believed I can learn — and do —anything.

That doesn't mean it turns out perfect the first time. Jim still twitches when we remember a crooked bus wall, and we'll never forget the kitchen sink incident when I cut the main supply lines, thinking they were copper, only to find they were galvanized steel. Oops. No kitchen sink for Christmas, but we did get to take twelve trips to Lowe's in one day — the true twelve days of Christmas!

The only job we refused to DIY was installing the hook-up for the gas range (don't judge; we love to cook) because, well, gas is invisible and can kill you.

Fortunately, we've survived the rest, and every mistake has taught us something we've applied to the next project. Like so many things in life, there's a reward for failed attempts, and in this case, it made each new DIY undertaking just a little easier.

November 3, 2024

Fall Back into Fun: 7 Ways to Soothe Seasonal Sunday Scaries

Whether you enjoy cooking or not, it's a great time of year to whip up a new recipe. Cooking can be a therapeutic way to wrap up your Sunday and prepare you for the week, so try something new in the kitchen. Even if it comes out inedible, progress counts as practice. 😆

💡 Lesson: What can you experiment with in the kitchen this week?

Pink Floyd hoodie reporting for duty.

You've probably never cut a hole in the roof of a bus and, to be honest, neither have I. I totally made Jim do that part! But, I bet you've experienced the compounding effect of confidence through action simply by doing something you didn't feel you could do or had never attempted before.

I still remember my very first client — the one who slid her credit card across a coffee shop table in Denver while I tried to discreetly pick my jaw up off the floor. We still keep tabs on each other via LinkedIn, and I'm not entirely sure she knows she is the first person who ever paid me to support her in her career journey. Lucky for me, and everyone I've helped since, she was willing to take a chance on me…and so was I.

We all have to start somewhere, and that's the wonder of doing hard things. We develop a thicker skin, build up stronger skills, and stand a little taller when the next big undertaking presents itself.

Bid on a $100,000 project, so you can go after the $1M deal. Coach a vice president, and then move on to the C-Suite. Speak to a room of ten, so you step on the stage in front of one hundred.

Action first, confidence second. Not the other way around. Confidence doesn't show up before the work; it is built *by* the work. This isn't a chicken and the egg debate, folks. There's a clear order here, and if you don't believe me, just think about anyone who has started the first job out of college, changed careers, started a business, or hell, brought a fragile infant home from the hospital for the first time. Every single one of those requires us to do something we've never done before.

The only way we prove to ourselves we can do these things is to take a chance on ourselves, put one foot in front of the other, and let the compounding effects bleed over into other areas of life and work.

If I can wire a full electrical panel in a bus, I can architect a curriculum for a coaching program. If I can troubleshoot a slanted floor on the fly, I can build a business from scratch. If I can figure out cabinetry angles, I can facilitate a two-day leadership retreat in France!

Learning is neat, isn't it?

Humans are, by nature, inquisitive creatures,[22] and it's that very curiosity that pushes us to take action before we know everything we need to know. Before we're ready.

Of course, we rarely hit it out of the park on the first swing. Inevitably, we'll strike out way more than we'll make contact. Landing a dream job, understanding what sets us apart, and discovering our purpose are things that rarely happen straight out of college. We simply don't know enough yet — about the world or ourselves.

But over time, we build.

We build skills, knowledge, and awareness — and eventually, it'll connect. We'll hit one out of the park.

Tile a backsplash, and then gut a kitchen. Paint one wall in a rental, and then paint an entire house (so we could buy it). We created a house in a bus, and then realized we were

22 Kennedy, J.J. "The Psychology and Neuroscience of Curiosity." *Psychology Today,* 2023. Yes, your brain really does love asking "Why?"

building a life. None of it was perfect. But all of it counted, and that's the point.

The lesson isn't in perfection. It's in perseverance. Action over anxiety. Movement over paralysis. Done is better than perfect.

Small moves. Inertia. Learn, adjust, and then take another step.

That's the trap most of us fall into. We wait for confidence before we act on the new job, the promotion, the business idea. We want to know it's going to work and pre-plan every step to get to that level of certainty. But if you wait for those conditions to be met, you'll be waiting for a long time.

Confidence rarely comes first. Action does.

The same principle applies whether we're cutting a hole in the roof of a bus or raising a hand for a project at work. Whether tiling our first backsplash or leading our first team. Whether we're taking on our first client or our fiftieth.

Most of us forget that confidence isn't a prerequisite; it's a byproduct. We want to believe there's some magical moment when we'll feel "ready" for that big presentation, the risky career move, the first client, or the next stage of leadership, but readiness doesn't arrive in advance. It's built through the very act of *doing the things*.

Every mis-cut piece of wood, late-night Lowe's run, and paint spill taught me something I applied to the next grand endeavor. Challenging myself to learn new physical activities,

May 18, 2025

22 Years, 1 Hard Hat, and 0 Sunday Scaries Later

We hear it all the time: knowledge is power.

Now I know how you gain that knowledge: doing.

As a college student, I thought confidence came from a textbook, which is only natural when you go through the rigor of a top engineering education.

Since then, I've found that bias for action, a willingness to try new things, and curiosity are just as, if not more important, to building knowledge and confidence as any academic setting.

 Lesson: Confidence is earned in motion, not in theory.

like skiing at 41 and mountain biking at 42.8, showed me I am capable of tackling new things. From surviving a failed box jump at the CrossFit gym to living through the hours-long frustration of unknotting a fly line, I built confidence.

That confidence not only carried over. It stacked. But I'm not telling you to run out and rent a jackhammer. In your world, it might be clicking "submit" on the job application even when you don't meet every qualification. Hitting publish on the post you've been sitting on for months. Leading a team meeting or taking the stage for the first time.

Every action, even the clumsy, imperfect, leave-scars-on-the-elbows kind, becomes a deposit in the confidence bank…and that financial institution pays dividends! Each attempt makes the next one a little less scary. Each scar becomes proof that we survived the leap, and we start to understand that setbacks aren't detrimental to our success.

Failure, as discussed in Chapter One, generally translates to "learning experience."

This is what many of us misunderstand about confidence. It isn't necessarily a personality trait. It's a skill, and it builds one micro-action at a time.

Unfortunately, we have the tendency to wait and resist. The desire for perfection in us turns to procrastination as a stall tactic. We avoid the anxiety of potentially being bad at something by not doing it at all. We tell ourselves we'll move when the conditions are right: when the kids are out of the house, there's more money in the bank, when the five-point plan is tied up with a pretty bow and a cherry on top.

Spoiler alert: there will always be something else that needs to happen before we feel "permitted" to try. That waiting will rob us of the very confidence we're hoping to build. Even worse, waiting for the right time can create resentment and regret and keep us from living up to the potential we have in this one life.

That doesn't mean we go from the bunny hill to hiking Highlands Bowl[23] in the same weekend. No! All we need to do is take a step. However small. Act first, then let confidence catch up.

*My favorite and forever mountain buddy
atop Highlands Bowl, New Year's Day 2022*

23 Highlands Bowl: Aspen's legendary hike-to terrain, complete with 782 vertical feet of lung-burning "fun" that separates the locals from the rest of us mere mortals. No oxygen. Never-ending Type II fun!

Action > Anxiety

As we've established, Sunday Scaries thrive in ambiguity. When we let ourselves linger in the gap between knowing and doing, we invite in the dread and usher out our dreams.

I'm behind.
I'm underqualified.
Everyone's life is better than mine.
I don't deserve it.
I'm not enough.

We've all been there — should-ing all over ourselves, letting the Sunday Scaries whisper not-so-sweet nothings in our ears.

Know what shuts it up?

Not perfection. Not permission. Not controlling every variable. Not doing more.

Intentional action. One brave, imperfect step at a time.

And in that moment, we take the power back from the Sunday Scaries. We step out of the cycle of dreading Mondays, chasing Fridays, and promising ourselves "someday."

Because there is no "someday." There is only today.

So stop waiting. Stop wondering. Stop wishing you were ready. Stop waiting for someone else to hand you permission.

You already have it.
This is your life.
This is your move.
Take it.

That's what it means to live *Scary Good* — to discover the life that's waiting on the other side of anxiety, fear, and other people's expectations. A life where intention leads the way, purpose clears the path, and confidence keeps your foot on the gas to the most incredible destination you could ever arrive at.

No More Mondays Companion Episodes

The Unexpected Entrepreneur: Finding Purpose in the Digital Age with Mark Lebrun *(February 24, 2025)*

Start With What You've Got: Resourcefulness Equals Freedom with Navid Moosa *(June 2, 2025)*

The Power of Storytelling: Building Authentic Brands and Human Connections with Ryan Koral *(August 4, 2025)*

Chapter 12

HUMANS STILL MATTER
Life Beyond the Sunday Scaries

"The meaning of life is to find your gift. The
purpose of life is to give it away."

Pablo Picasso

I WORE A shirt that just says, **HUMAN.** on it in the airport
recently. I had several of them made to wear each day of an AI
conference, where I was a keynote speaker…talking about how
to be human. Appropriate, don't ya think? I thought so, which
is why I decided to rock one the minute I stepped out of my
house for the trip.

I lost count of how many people smiled at me (and stared at
my boobs) while I was walking through the airport. It was like we
were all in on an inside joke. The TSA guy at our tiny mountain
airport looked at me and said, "We need more of those."

Yes, sir. Yes, we do.

Humans. Still. Matter.

So simple. A word we all share. The very literal definition of every single person I walked by, yet it seemed so noticeable. Unique. Foreign, even. It reinforced something for me:

We're all just people trying to do our best in a world that is becoming more disconnected and divided by the minute.

Maybe that's why I made the shirt in the first place. Sure, it's a marketing stunt, but it's also a reminder. The world is moving fast. We celebrate progress, performance, and productivity more than anything else. The tradeoff? Somewhere along the way, we stopped celebrating people. It seems as if humanity is only universally acknowledged at two points in life: when we're born and when we die.

Sorry, the book took a morbid turn there, but honestly, doesn't that seem kinda messed up? When did we trade connection, humanity, and heart for efficiency and dollar signs?

Apparently, it took a cotton-blend shirt with four-inch letters to help me realize what I've been trying to do for the past fifteen years of my life (and the past eleven chapters of this book). Maybe that's what all of this has been leading to: **the reminder that humans still matter**.

Maybe that's why this all feels so full circle to me; why writing this book was something I could wait no longer to do. The compulsion to get this all out of my head and into your hands was too potent, too relevant for this snapshot in time.

I'm part of a generation that grew up analog and now lives digital, old enough to remember life before Wi-Fi, but young enough to adopt every new app without needing to call tech support. In fact, I *am* tech support (Hi, Mom).

From playing in the dirt and coming home when Mom yelled out the front door, to smacking the side of the television to get a fourth channel, I could still be dumbfounded at the lack of cords on phones nowadays if I let myself. That monster

October 12, 2025

A.I. Can't Fix Your Sunday Scaries (Yet 😛)

Stay human, on purpose. It's just that simple.

Our busy lives can trigger autopilot. Inboxes, algorithms, endless scrolls; it's really easy to stare at the screen in your hand and not the human sitting on the couch next to you.

Being intentional about humanity means remembering why you started, who you serve, and what lights you up.

💡 Lesson: Humans Still Matter.

of a desktop computer I hauled up three flights of stairs to my sorority room was so beastly it probably *did* cause lifelong sciatica — and all sixty-four megs of its RAM glory are now as laughable as the floppy disk that came before it. We're not even going to talk about Napster.

And now, we're doing it all over again with artificial intelligence. If you're a fellow member of the *Star Wars* generation (1977 - 1983), you feel it, too. We built our careers "the old-fashioned way," only to find ourselves learning how to coexist with something that can mimic us...but, at least for now, not *be* us.

Even if you were born outside of those years, you know things have changed. Over the past two decades, we've watched the working world shift more than it did in the fifty years before it. Heck, maybe even the prior fifteen. We've gone from cubicles and punch cards to Zoom calls and hybrid offices. Ladders have been traded for lifestyle. Careers now branch more than climb.

Suits are even a thing of the past; well, at least the bottom half is. We've traded titles for meaning and pensions for purpose. Through all of that change, something unexpected happened: **we got agency.**

At one point in a few earlier pages, we talked about how we have more control over our lives than we think we do, and certainly more than we exercise. More of us than ever are starting to leverage it. We're starting to look less at "What do I do?" and more at "Why do I do this?"

The data backs up that trend. Multiple recent surveys[24] show today's workforce is prioritizing meaning as much as money, with nearly nine in ten Gen Z and Millennials saying purpose is more important to their job satisfaction. Show me an algorithm that predicted that thirty years ago!

Regardless of age, I talk to people every day who are realizing they don't have to keep doing what they've been doing for the past twenty years *for* the next twenty years. From finding more meaning in their work to better cultural alignment, satisfaction, time at home, whatever the driver, it seems we're done living and working in two different compartments.

We're ready to merge it all. We are past the days of living life in the ten minutes left after work, dinner, and putting kids to bed. It's time to design the life we want and find (or create) the career that supports it, instead of the other way around.

It is time for integration.

Generations before us didn't have this luxury. They didn't question the Sunday Scaries because they didn't have a name for them — they just plain old didn't *have* them. Work was work. Clock in, clock out. Get home in time for dinner with a side of Jell-O and Cool Whip. Life was basically a countdown to retirement, and in those days, retirement meant freedom to live.

---

24 McKinsey & Company, "Help Your Employees Find Purpose — or Watch Them Leave," 2020; *Deloitte Global Gen Z & Millennial Survey*, 2024/2025; *Randstad Workmonitor*, 2025. Apparently, my friend Mike Kim was on to something with that whole *economy of meaning* thing.

That's not judgment; it's context. Work, in the past, was a matter of survival. I mean, go back even further, and it was literally a matter of life and death. Farm for food, or starve. Keep the oxen healthy enough to cross the Oregon Trail, or die of dysentery.

Today, it can be so much more. We're living longer, and our careers are stretching right along with us. We have more energy and stamina in our older years, with a drive to continue contributing to the world, and let's face it...the death of the pension means we *need* to keep contributing to the world.

But this isn't about need.

We're waking up to the idea that maybe this whole "life is too short" thing should also mean "life's too important to waste."

The Sunday Scaries were never about dreading Monday; they were about disconnection, misalignment, and misplaced priorities. They're the symptoms of a system that told us our worth was in our output and that peace could wait until the weekend. Even better if it waited until age 62.5.

We don't live there anymore, and in writing this book, I realized I arrived at that conclusion a little earlier than many of my peers. Call me the trailblazer that ChatGPT always wants to refer to me as, or call me crazy. The pragmatism of a Gen X-er, combined with the hopefulness of a Millennial, collided on a journey where I challenged this norm before it was considered normal to do so.

It hasn't been easy. In fact, most of it has been downright hard, but I know I'm a better person for it, and I also know it was all necessary — the learning, the preparation, the perspective. I needed it to navigate my own life, and I needed to write this book. To make a difference. To find my purpose. To make sure humans still matter.

We're in the moment to design something different. Everything we've learned up to now has been preparing us to lead with intention, live with purpose, and integrate the two so seamlessly that we can't tell where work ends and life begins.

That's what Scary Good really means.

It's not the absence of fear or failure. It doesn't mean life is perfect. It's the presence of meaning. It's knowing that there's life beyond the Sunday Scaries, and we're no longer competing to get to the finish line.

Scary Good is an invitation to become, to own, and to accept your whole self. The one who has amazing gifts to share with the world, potential to live up to, and impact to leave behind.

I don't know about you, but I want to live in *that* reality as long as possible.

The best time to plant a shade tree was twenty years ago.
The next best time? Today.

Jane Goodall, who passed away the day before I started penning this chapter, once said, "What you do makes a difference, and you have to decide what kind of difference you want to make."

For someone who dedicated her life to understanding another species, she understood ours better than most. Maybe that's because she knew what so many of us seemed to forget: it's not the size or scale of our impact. It's the decision to make it at all.

I think about that a lot. At one point, life circumstances forced me into hiding. To stay and play small, and during that time, I felt as if I wasn't permitted to make a difference. Wasn't worthy of having an impact. Shamed into thinking I didn't deserve to be considered a good human.

Then I realized that was not only a giant load of *bull*, but it was also the exact opposite of how I should be thinking.

Purpose isn't a goal. Impact isn't earned. And meaning certainly isn't a prize we get to unwrap after completing our thirty years of service. (*Hey, where's my pin?*)

We often hear it said: The journey is the destination.
Another cliché.
Another truth.

If Picasso was right, and the meaning of life is to find and give away our gifts, then I have to believe that's also where we discover life beyond the Sunday Scaries. It's the byproduct of everything we've talked about in these pages — alignment, courage, authenticity, gratitude, grit, confidence — all working together. It's not a big bang, but an arrival. And every micro-moment where we choose to act instead of avoid gets us there.

It's the collection of brave choices that make up our one human life.

Assemble the pieces, and you'll arrive at your awakening. No more living in conflict with ourselves. No more dividing who we are from what we do. We lead the same way we live, and we live the same way we lead: intentionally, imperfectly, unapologetically human.

That's what living *beyond* the Sunday Scaries really looks like. It's not about balance; it's about equilibrium. Not about control; about contentment. Not about perfection; about peace.

Once we stop compartmentalizing our lives, when work and life, ambition and rest, progress and presence all have space to coexist, we become whole. We become our *realest* version of ourselves. We live **authentically**.

This is the integration we've been building toward, where all the lessons converge. We realize we were never trying to "fix" ourselves; we were learning to remember who we already are. The world likes to get in the way of that, to try to make us forget, to lose track, to submit to what the world tells us we are.

Sorry, world: I dissent.

Maybe the hardest part about living beyond the Sunday Scaries isn't knowing *what* to do next; it's maintaining the conviction to keep doing it. To keep showing up with curiosity and commitment. To remember where we've come from. To keep choosing alignment when convenience tempts us back into autopilot. So start small.

Choose one thing that reminds you you're *alive*, not busy, not productive, but *alive*.

A morning walk without earbuds.
A handwritten letter to someone instead of a text.
Trying to cook something you've never tried before.
A conversation where you listen instead of replying.
Running errands without your phone.
A puzzle on the coffee table.
A meal away from the TV.

These are the moments where alignment becomes practice, where purpose stops being a concept and starts becoming a habit, where we remember what's most important to us and remain present to it.

Sometimes, we need to revert to an older version. Sometimes, we need a system reset. Sometimes, we need analog.

That's how humans stay human.

I've spent the past decade of my life working to become who I knew I could, wanted, and was meant to be, and I'll never be finished. There will always be work to do, things to learn, and challenges to navigate in the journey to becoming the best possible version of myself. That's the beauty of this little thing called life.

But maybe, just maybe, in your own way, you're ready to start the exploration, too. Because at the end of the day, no matter how fast the world moves, how advanced the tech gets, or how digital we become, one truth remains:

Humans still matter.
You still matter.

Take the gift you've been given.

Share it. Live it. Lean into it. Lead with intention.
Live with purpose.

And remember — the life you're building isn't just good.

It's *Scary* Good.

No More Mondays Companion Episodes

Find Your Economy of Meaning with Mike Kim
(November 2, 2025)

Break the Belief Barrier: Purpose-Driven Growth with
Quinn Hardwood *(July 28, 2025)*

On Gaining Clarity and Embracing Discomfort:
an Eye-Opening Conversation with Rusty Gaillard
(October 21, 2024)

Building a Better You with Carole Stizza *(October 14, 2024)*

Acknowledgements

NO BOOK IS ever ever really written alone, and this one is no exception. *Scary Good* exists because of the people who have consistently shown up for me, asked the right questions (which aren't always easy ones), and provided the love, encouragement, and hugs to help me through the good times… and the bad

To my parents, **Soni and Floyd**, you modeled resilience long before I ever knew I'd need it. I wouldn't be who I am today without the faith, love, and values you instilled in me.

To **Kathy Sparrow**, whose editorial guidance undoubtedly gave me the clarity and courage to create what you just read. Thank you for your wisdom, partnership, and for fly fishing with me IRL!

To **all the friends**, from my fellow gym rats to those who share our street, and especially those who push me on the pedals, you make the world complete for this former engineer *who loves people*.

To the coaches, leaders, and clients I've had the privilege of working with over the years — especially to the incredible humans inside **The Modern Coach** community — your stories, courage, and willingness to grow have inspired more pages than you'll ever realize.

To every single guest who has given their time and wisdom to me and the air waves via **No More Mondays** podcast, thank you. Whether you're included in these pages or not, know you helped not only shape a movement. You helped shape me.

To **Justin Schenck**, for pouring into people with the same heart (and healthy dose of sarcasm) as me, and for writing a foreword that made my eyes a little misty.

To **Meredith Schurch**, for casually mentioning to me one day in 2021 that I should start a newsletter about the Sunday Scaries.

To **Kristen Peele**, thank you for making the Sunday Scaries come alive each week for almost two-and-a-half years. You helped evolve them into what they are today, and that is exactly what inspired the direction of this book.

To every reader of the **Sunday Scaries Newsletter**. You are the OG crew who proved that honesty, humor, and a little reflection can change the trajectory of a week, a mind, and a life. You sparked this book.

And finally, to **anyone who has ever felt stuck** between who you are and who you know you can be: you were on my mind with every keystroke. May these pages help you feel seen, understood, and a little more human.

No More Mondays
Listening Guide

Throughout *Scary Good*, you'll find episode pairings designed to complement each chapter. Here's the full list for easy access:

Chapter 1

Embracing Imperfection: How to Overcome the Pitfalls of Perfectionism with Dr. Greg Chasson *(December 3, 2024)*

Struggling with Imposter Syndrome? Learn how to Overcome the Imposter with Kris Kelso *(December 6, 2023)*

Stop the Proving, Pleasing, and Perfecting with Heather Whelpley *(October 12, 2022)*

Chapter 2

The Quest for Happiness: How to Find Meaning in Our Fast-Paced World with Ashish Kothari *(July 26, 2023)*

Walking in Purpose: How to Live and Grow in Alignment with Your Strengths with John Thompson, III *(March 22, 2023)*

How to Thrive in a Rapidly Changing World with John Saunders *(October 13, 2021)*

Chapter 7

How to Be Unforgettable, Without a Stage or Spotlight with Phil Mershon *(June 23, 2025)*

Deliberate Evolution: Burnout, Balance & The Ecology of Leadership with Dan Capello *(September 8, 2025)*

How Curiosity and Authenticity Fuel Entrepreneurship with Alyssa Nolte *(September 15, 2025)*

Chapter 8

Beat the Burnout: Living Stoked with Sarah Bettman *(February 28, 2024)*

A Chat with Our Favorite Predictor of Powder: Joel Gratz on Turning a Passion into a Business *(April 25, 2023)*

Fueling the Entrepreneurial Engine: The Power of Health and Wellness with Mark Gray *(November 18, 2024)*

From Burnout to Brilliance: How Creativity and Fun Can Transform Work and Life with Mike Brennan *(January 27, 2025)*

Chapter 9

The Power of Community: Build Connection, Courage, and Freedom with Vincent Pugliese *(April 28, 2025)*

Say Yes: Building Careers and Communities Through Connection with Greg Wasserman *(September 22, 2025)*

Humanizing Communication: How to Speak With People *(Not At Them) with Jason Raitz (October 13, 2025)*

Chapter 10

How Will You Be Great Today? With Andre Young
(May 12, 2025)

Leadership in the Making: The Learn-It-All Advantage with Damon Lembi *(June 16, 2025)*

From Command to Connection: Modern Leadership with Christopher Sprague *(September 29, 2025)*

Chapter 11

The Unexpected Entrepreneur: Finding Purpose in the Digital Age with Mark Lebrun *(February 24, 2025)*

Start With What You've Got: Resourcefulness Equals Freedom with Navid Moosa *(June 2, 2025)*

The Power of Storytelling: Building Authentic Brands and Human Connections with Ryan Koral *(August 4, 2025)*

Chapter 12

Find Your Economy of Meaning with Mike Kim
(November 2, 2025)

Break the Belief Barrier: Purpose-Driven Growth with Quinn Hardwood *(July 28, 2025)*

On Gaining Clarity and Embracing Discomfort: an Eye-Opening Conversation with Rusty Gaillard *(October 21, 2024)*

Building a Better You with Carole Stizza *(October 14, 2024)*

Scan the code for podcast episodes,
resources, and to connect with Angie!

About the Author

ANGIE CALLEN is an author, speaker, coach, and most importantly, the authentic human behind **Career Benders, Inc.** and **The Modern Coach**, where she helps people build meaningful careers, resilient businesses, and purpose-driven lives. A former engineer turned entrepreneur, Angie blends sharp analytical thinking with humor, practicality, and a very human approach to growth and leadership.

She is the host of the **No More Mondays** podcast, creator of the **Sunday Scaries Newsletter**, and the developer of multiple coaching and certification programs for career professionals and coaches alike. Her work focuses on authenticity, values-based decision-making, and redefining success on your own terms.

Angie's career path has included engineering, nonprofit leadership, entrepreneurship, mountain-town living, and more than a few detours that became defining moments — many of which you'll find in this book. Her mission is simple: to remind people that humans still matter, and that a fulfilling life is built through intentional choices, not accidental circumstances.

Originally from Pennsylvania, Angie now lives in **Glenwood Springs, Colorado**, with her husband Jim, their rescue dog Steve, and Tacocat, the world's most charismatic 16-pound "dog-cat." When she's not coaching, writing, or recording a podcast episode, you'll find her mountain biking, skiing, or enjoying the magic of everyday life in the mountains.

You can learn more about Angie's work, coaching programs, and writing at **angiecallen.com**.

Get the
Sunday Scaries Newsletter

THE NEWSLETTER THAT inspired this book is alive and well — and waiting for you.

Every Sunday, I send one short, honest, human message designed to help you reset, reflect, and start the week feeling a little more grounded and a lot more capable.

Get on the list here:

scarygoodread.com/sundayscaries

Follow My Adventures

HANG OUT WITH me on social where you can get an even better glimpse into mountain adventure, free-range adulthood, and what it's like to life your best life at 6,000 feed above sea level!

LinkedIn → linkedin.com/in/angiecallen

Facebook → facebook.com/angiecallen and facebook.com/careerbenders

Instagram → @angieonanadvenure and @careerbenders

Podcast → nomoremondays.info

Threads → @angieoneanadventure and @careerbenders

Youtube → youtube.com/@careerbenders

You can also find everything linked on my website:
www.angiecallen.com

www.ingramcontent.com/pod-product-compliance
Lightning Source LLC
Chambersburg PA
CBHW051611120626
46551CB00014B/1750